Praise for Heart of a Lion

"This is a touching and uplifting true story about a boy named John Paul, who has half a heart, but who lives with more heart and soul than just about any kid you will ever meet. John Paul rocks, and so does this book.

—James Patterson

Heart of a Lion is a heart-warming and emotional true-life adventure, involving a child's battle against formidable odds, his parents' unrelenting support, and help from higher sources.

—Rob MacGregor

Author of *Indiana Jones and the Last Crusade*
and seven other Indy novels

An inspirational story of a family's relentless fight to save their son from a devastating diagnosis. Their journey inspires hope.

—Alan Lavine and Gail Liberman,
Dow Jones columnist and authors of
Quick Steps to Financial Stability, Que Books.

A story of a child who beat the odds. We hope to put a smile on your face. "Go Big Blue."

New York Giants–Super Bowl Champ

John Paul's sparkling brown eyes and endearing smile radiate joy. This book radiates hope, love and endurance.

Bill Parcells
Super Bowl Coach

HEART
of a
LION

HEART
of a
LION

DEREK
GEORGE

TATE PUBLISHING
AND ENTERPRISES, LLC

Published by Tate Publishing & Enterprises, LLC
127 E. Trade Center Terrace | Mustang, Oklahoma 73064 USA
1.888.361.9473 | www.tatepublishing.com

Tate Publishing is committed to excellence in the publishing industry. The company reflects the philosophy established by the founders, based on Psalm 68:11,
"The Lord gave the word and great was the company of those who published it."

Published in the United States of America

ISBN: 978-1-62024-329-9
Biography & Autobiography / Personal Memoirs
12.04.16

*To my wife, Annette, my son, John Paul, and
my family, thanks for all the support*

You can be born into a nightmare, but
God can usher you into a dream.

—Tyler Perry

Acknowledgments

There are many people to thank when it comes to writing this book. I begin with my son, John Paul, the love of my life. Thank you for blessing my life each day.

And my wife, Annette, for your dedication and unending assistance, without whom this book never would have been possible.

To our parents, Tommy and Robena Wagner and Dolour and Lettie George, thanks for being our solid ground during the many mountains and valleys.

To Cecilia, Father Gary and Gerard, my siblings, thanks for your constant faith, reassurance and always being there.

And in memory of Annette's sister and brother, Debbie and Barry, who through their actions taught me the attribute of fortitude and the magnitude of a smile.

Also, to all the people who have touched John Paul's life in their own special way. The Kirsch, McKinney, Pierce, and Schindler family, Tyler Perry, Carole Wurst, Erik Compton, Coach Ream, Don Smith, Jack Nicklaus, Jane Seymour, Michael Clayton, Tiffany Beasley, Kathy Brown, Dr. Bayron, Father O'Shea, Chrissi Deutsch, Debbie Guinn, the Friday morning breakfast group, our Passionist Priests, Maggie Kirsch for the amazing cover photo, all our families, friends and to the many people who prayed and continue to pray for John Paul around the world.

And finally, thanks to everyone else who is a part of John Paul's life, each of you have made such a positive impact.

Foreword

The decision to become a parent is monumental in the lives of most couples. In theory, it should be attempted after lengthy discussions and deliberation; although, this is rarely the case. Most of us stumble through life in a cavalier fashion with little regard for the consequences of our actions.

Ideally, each family would start in a stable environment with the fiscal ability to care for a child. We would be in excellent health of mind and body before attempting such a daunting task. However, most children are conceived out of the love of two persons, which is ultimately the most important element in human existence.

Each parent has notions about their future child's characteristics. We all, in our naive approach, view our baby as perfect in all aspects. The more harsh reality is that term pregnancies are often complicated by congenital malformations in 3% of pregnancies. Of this group, the largest number, are children with congenital heart disease, constituting 1% of all live births. Hypoplastic left heart defect is one of the most serious of these conditions which is almost universally fatal without surgical intervention soon after birth.

This book is a remarkable tale of a boy who has captured my heart and those of hundreds of others who have cared for him during his sixteen years of life.

His quirky smile and sense of humor are his greatest attributes. He has endured more pain, discomfort and uncertainty in his brief life than most 60 year olds. Despite all odds, he has grown and lives a life akin to most other children his age. Most of all, he reminds us of the fact that being a parent can be the most heart wrenching and conversely the most rewarding of tasks. Each child has unlimited potential and it is up to us as relatives, friends and parents to rejoice in them as individuals.

—Dr. Richard Kirsch

Author's Note

The cover photograph of Heart of a Lion is profound when you view it from a faith-based prospective. My arms and body encompass my son, John Paul, to express my unconditional love and offer him the security of my unwavering embrace. How wonderful is the superior and swathing embrace provided by God? His perpetual and tender love enfolds us, providing a steadfast shelter.

My family has experienced that divine shrouding on many occasions since the birth of my son. It's not just His embrace but the miracles provided by His everlasting encompassing shield.

Wikipedia defines

Miracle: A miracle often denotes an event attributed to divine intervention.

A miracle...

How else can John Paul's life be described? He isn't supposed to be here... He wasn't supposed to live beyond birth... There wasn't supposed to be hope... That was the unwavering consensus of doctors from prestigious medical institutions. These accords were made on assumptions, based on the evidence, but failed to consider one crucial factor: the power of God's divine intervention.

The presence of God is like air; it surrounds us... Give thanks with every breath

Summer of 1994

The Paraclete

I close my eyes, only for a moment, and the moment's gone. All my dreams pass before my eyes, a curiosity.

Kansas–Dust in the Wind

John Paul saying his prayers

I lost count of the number of days my wife and I remained within the confines of the subdued environment; for us time stands still. I am locked in a prison of emotions, riding the rollercoaster of despair and hope.

It is nearing the end of June. My daily routine has not changed since the birth of my son, John Paul, on June the fourth.

Vigilantly, I remain by his bedside praying, hoping and watching for any signs of improvement.

The cardiologist, Dr. Renar, a tomboyish woman in her late thirties, approaches. She encourages Annette and I, as a doctor or nurse did everyday, to go home for the night and get some much needed rest. The answer is always the same: I do not want to leave for fear something might go wrong and I will not be around. Tonight she is persistent because John Paul's condition is more stable than it has been. I still remember her words, "Go home. Get a good night's sleep so you'll be refreshed when John Paul wakes up." I heed her advice with much apprehension.

As I start to leave I realize I am not sure how to get out of the hospital. The massive cold building has become home. The basics, a place to shower, a cot to sleep and a cafeteria to eat are provided, allowing Annette and I to maintain a twenty-four seven vigil with our son. Hand-in-hand Annette and I walk the corridors. Turning the corner I see a bright red exit sign. The closer I get to the door, the heavier my steps become. My emotions creep into my throat creating a lump. I feel guilty for leaving without my son in my arms.

Once home I fumble with the keys but finally unlock the door and enter the house. Annette hits the light switch. The first thing that catches my attention is a car seat, the only baby purchase made. Having a baby is so ordinary these days. The main focus is whether it is a boy or a girl or how to decorate the nursery. That is until the extraordinary happens; then the focus shifts to survival which engrosses me. Annette can't bear to look at the car seat; she avoids it and walks into the bedroom. I stand and stare. My thoughts reflect to my friend John whom I watched install his son's car seat, a feat that consumed more time and effort than he had allowed for. My hand traces the seat as I envision buckling John Paul in for his first ride.

I finally settle into bed and watch the ceiling fan slice the moonlit room. My thoughts never sway from my son, even in my deep slumber he is there. Around midnight the sound of a ringing phone pierces the darkness. At the echo of the first ring my stomach churns and nervousness tingles through my body. The voice on the other end confirms my worst fear: John Paul has taken a turn for the worse.

My feet hit the floor; a haze encircles me. My heart begins to pound; my hands start to shake. I don't remember getting dressed, but once behind the wheel of my car the adrenaline flows through my veins. I frantically whiz through every stoplight and stop sign with my hazard lights flashing. The car will not go fast enough. As I press the gas pedal, my leg trembles uncontrollably. I screech into a parking space; Annette and I make a mad dash for the door. As soon as the florescent lights and hospital smell filter around me, reality settles in. This may be the last time I see my son. I am in a race against time.

Annette and I enter the Pediatric ICU. I look at John Paul's bed; doctors and nurses surround the tiny crib. I start to walk over but when Dr. Renar sees me she approaches. She doesn't have to say a word; her usually upbeat attitude is void. The look on her face says it all. She explains John Paul's situation. His saturations (oxygen levels) are dropping fast, meaning his brain and body are being starved for air. The turmoil is taking a toll on his weak heart. It is doubtful his heart will withstand the pressure. She notes John Paul is barely alive and only has a one percent chance of surviving.

These words cause Annette's body to go limp. I pull her into me and try to remain strong, but I feel I am at the end of my rope. Thoughts swirl through my head like leaves on a blustery fall day. Why this innocent little boy? Why is he suffering so? Is this how it's going to end? Is a parent's worst fear happening to me?

The doctor explains that a jet ventilator capable of delivering two-hundred and sixty 'jet breaths' per minute is the last resource in trying to revive John Paul's oxygen levels. I watch as respiratory therapists wheel the huge jet ventilator by me and begin inserting the breathing tube into my son's fragile little body. Emotions begin to flow from my eyes. I feel so helpless.

A nurse places her arm around my shoulder. "Why don't you two stay in the waiting room down the hall. I'll come get you when respiratory finishes."

Before leaving ICU, I maneuver my way through the doctors and nurses; I have to let John Paul know I am with him. The hums of the machines are overpowering. I stand over his crib and soak up his every feature, jet black hair, long dark lashes, perfect little nose and cute chubby feet. Everything on the outside is so perfect; my only wish is the inside would be the same. Slowly I lean over, and whisper in his ear. "You're a tiger, keep fighting, and don't give up! I love you so much." Gently I kiss his head and start praying for a miracle.

Annette and I walk arm in arm, trying to steady each other's steps. The waiting room down the hall from ICU is no bigger than a walk-in closet. Five chairs line the wall. I sit in the second one. Annette sits down beside me in the one on the left, leaving the chair next to me on the right vacant. I didn't call any of our family, there hadn't been time. Annette and I sit alone in the middle of the night, holding hands and praying for our son. The small room heavy with fear and anxiety emits the illusion of a two-ton weight slowly closing in.

The hallway outside the open door, normally busy with doctors, interns, nurses and visitors passing by, is desolate in the wee hours of the morning.

Out of nowhere, an elderly black man in his eighties appears at the door. He is wearing dark brown pants, a white button-up short-sleeve shirt with a white tee underneath. I didn't recognize him, which is unusual as I have gotten to know most of the employees from being at the hospital around the clock. He has one hand on a large gray trashcan he had been pulling, and the other hand is rubbing his knee. "My knee is killing me; I need to take a seat for a few minutes," he said.

I don't take much notice of him. I keep my head bowed think-ing of my son. The man comes in and sit in the empty chair next to me and proceeds to rub both of his knees as he speaks.

"Family's real important." His voice is firm, yet soft and soothing.

"Yes, I know," I say not looking up.

He removes his right hand from his knee and places it on mine. As soon as his hand touches my leg a warm sensation radi-ates through me. I raise my head and stare at him. I am captivated by his eyes; they are brilliant blue, the color of the Caribbean Sea. His slightly creased ebony skin accents the hues and his gaze penetrates deep, offering me serenity.

He said, "My son, you have a child in there."

I answered, "Yes, but it doesn't look good."

With surety he said, "Don't worry, everything is going to be fine."

I thought to myself, *who is this guy and why is he telling me this with such conviction?*

The words barely leave his mouth when suddenly the nurse rushes to the doorway. "Hurry, come quick!" she exclaimed. Annette and I run out the door and follow her to ICU expecting the worse. As I enter, Dr. Renar is standing in the middle of the room shaking her head, not in disgust, but rather with a smile on her face. When I see the smile I feel weightless.

"I can't understand this!" she said.

I stand in shock, utter disbelief. "What happened?" I ask.

"John Paul's saturations have shot back up and his functions are returning to normal. We did everything humanly possible to make this work, but this miracle could have only come from one place." Her eyes gaze upward as her hands point toward heaven.

Suddenly I realize divine intervention has interceded for John Paul. I think of the elderly man with the Caribbean blue eyes who just told me everything was going to be okay. I have to find this man to tell him the good news. I make a mad dash out of

ICU and run down the hall to the waiting room. It is empty. My heart pounds as I run down the corridor. I look in every room, but I can't find him. Exhausted I run back into ICU and ask the nurses about the custodian who works the night shift. I give a detailed description of him, but they stand dumbfounded. They have never seen the gentleman I described; furthermore I am told custodians do not work in the middle of the night.

Bewildered I slowly walk back over to John Paul; the warm sensation delivered by the man still remains. I reach down and place my index finger into John Paul's hand and think of the words spoken: "Don't worry, everything is going to be fine." In the remaining days and weeks at the hospital I never saw him again. There are days that I sit back and relive those moments: anxiety followed by elation, the look on the doctor's face and the way her hands and eyes shot up above. When I think of the old man, his words, his touch, goose bumps consume my entire body. Angels wear many faces and can appear in the oddest places. In my wildest dreams I never imagined a blue-eyed angel delivering hope and comfort in my darkest hour. I remain in awe at what happened. How I wish I would have spoken to him more, but one thing is for certain- to this day, in troubling times the warmth of his touch still pervades me, indicating his presence.

Chapter One

Fear

Fear is something to be moved through, not something to be turned from.

Peter McWilliams

John Paul ready for the big Easter Egg Hunt

Easter 1997

"On your mark, get set, go!" My neighbor shouts, signaling the start of the Easter Egg Hunt.

John Paul, wearing blue plaid shorts, a white shirt, and red suspenders with a red bowtie, attempts to make a dash for the

eggs. He tugs at my hand.   He looks up, his brown eyes sparkling. "Let me go, daddy!" It is hard to let go.   I want him in
my protective zone.   I slowly release my grip from our entwined
hands. He runs away.   I stare, unable to believe he is here.

My mind reels back to the day he was born.   Anticipation
was my shadow for nine months. Wonderment replaces expec-
tancy when he arrives. The sheer miracle of birth transforms me.
The nurse places him in my arms. I barely have time to commit
his delicate features to memory before he is whisked into a crib.
Elation turns to sorrow in a matter of minutes. I watch his tiny
body, become overshadowed by machines and IVs. I feel light-
headed and weak. The emotions of unconditional love grip my
heart. He is so helpless. What lies ahead for him? Dear God,
what will he have to endure? The doctors say he will not survive,
but I have to give him a chance. I have to give him a chance!

October 1993

Annette and I wait eight years to have a child. To most people
that's an eternity. The question asked repeatedly from family
and friends is *when*? Their curiosity doesn't faze us. We are
young with good jobs, but deep down there is a personal reason
for waiting. Annette's brother and sister both developed a serious genetic disease in their later teen years. This fatal disease left
them prisoners in their own bodies. Although Annette did not
develop the disease, she is still able to pass the recessive gene
to our children. This possibility quietly hinders our desire, but
finally after being told the odds are in our favor we decide to try.
In late October 1993 the most asked question finally receives an
answer. The popular statement following our exciting news: *You
have no idea how your life is going to change*. We soon find out.

January 1994

January 3,1994 excitement filters through the room. Annette and
I watch the technician initiate our first sonogram. We converse
back and forth about Christmas and how happy our families are

anticipating our new arrival. Suddenly, normal small-talk ceases. The technician pauses. She looks closer at the monitor. The silence consumes me and I ask, "Is everything okay?" The technician keeps her eyes on the monitor. "I'm sorry I'm not allowed to discuss the sonogram. A report will be sent to your doctor. He will be in touch." The thrill of the moment slips. Fear enters. We leave the hospital depleted, wondering what is wrong.

Have you ever felt someone needs you, but you can't explain why? The following day around lunchtime, this sensation pushes me from work to Annette's office. Exiting the elevator I hear hysterical sobs. My steps hasten. The closer I get to Annette's office the clearer the cry becomes. I reach the door. My body freezes. Her body is slouched over in a chair; her head rests in her hands. Her body is shaking uncontrollably. Margaret, a friend, stands by her side and tries to console her. A thousand thoughts surge through my mind.

"What's wrong?"

The sound of my voice throws Annette into my arms. She buries her head in my chest. Slowly she looks up. Tears stream down her cheeks. Her blue eyes accented by smudged mascara.

"Dr. Donner just called, he said something's wrong with the baby's heart. He said the baby will need a pacemaker at birth."

There are ways news of this caliber should be delivered. By phone, at work, isn't one of them. The audacity! Somewhere along the way some doctors have lost one of the most important concepts of doctoring: compassion.

Dr. Donner declined to give a diagnosis, only the number of an expert in the field Dr. Vega, a doctor at Forest Physicians. The full scope of the diagnosis will not be known until we are able to see the specialist.

It's amazing, when faced with adversity, how the human mind kicks into overdrive and reinstates some sanity. We begin to rationalize. *Maybe the technician made a mistake, besides Dr.*

Donner would have called us into his office if it were serious. Maybe we are overreacting. For two days our emotions fluctuate.

The news on January 6, 1994, Annette's birthday, is life-altering. The thirty- minute drive to Dr. Vega's office feels like two hours. Inside the massive building, I suddenly realize the severity of our situation.

Annette and I enter and prepare for the sonogram. The cold dark room only reinforces our fears. A man in green scrubs and a white jacket enters. He is medium height with salt and pepper hair with small black lenses framing his dark eyes. He isn't alone. An entire crew of residents, clad in the same scrubs and jackets follow. Suddenly I feel Annette and our unborn child are on display. I grab her hand and squeeze it tightly. Introductions are brief. Minutes later the scan begins. Dr. Vega studies and points at the screen. The residents lean for a closer look. This continues for sometime. Finally, he gazes over his glasses.

"Did Dr. Donner explain your baby's situation?"

"He told my wife something was wrong with the baby's heart and a pacemaker would probably be needed."

He clears his throat. "It's very serious. There is no positive news to give. Your baby has a rare condition called Hypoplastic Left Heart. The left side of the heart is dead." He pauses. "The baby is fine in the womb but once born, he or she will die." He states in matter of fact tone.

I think to myself, *did he just say die?* "What happened to the pacemaker?" I ask.

"A pacemaker will not help. The only way your baby will survive is with a heart transplant. Even that is a long shot."

My mind reels and tries to process. The only life our baby is going to have is in the womb. I look at Annette lying on the table, exposed, wanting to express the emotions building with each word exiting the doctor's mouth. A knock on the door cuts the tension. A small man with khaki pants, an olive green shirt and tie enters.

Dr. Vega introduces Annette and I to Dr. Penski from Pediatric Cardiology. After the two doctors review the scan, Annette and I follow Dr. Penski to his office. We sit across the desk from the doctor in a state of shock. I keep looking at Annette. Weeks before she glowed with happiness. I can't help but wonder how she will endure this ordeal. The maternal bond is already there. How will she cope as the baby grows, knowing the destiny? I think about the surprise baby shower the ladies at her office have planned. This celebration of new beginning has to be canceled. Also the decorating of the nursery must cease. Anger builds as I imagine a nursery full of everything except a baby. The house will remain the same. There will be no reminders of what could have been. I think of all the genetic testing endured to make sure neither were carriers of the gene that incapacitated Annette's brother and sister. But something totally different, the heart, the most vital organ has not formed properly. How on earth will we endure?

Side by side, hand in hand, we listen. Nods acknowledge the doctor's words, but comprehension is null.

"Is there any hope for survival?" I ask.

The doctor shakes his head, "No, not really. This condition almost always is fatal. Without a sonogram this disease can go undetected. A Hypoplastic baby, at birth, looks no different from any other. Many times mother and baby are released from the hospital. A few days later the baby dies at home because the hole allowing blood flow closes up. We will do everything we can but..."

Annette starts to cry. I am emotional too, but I remain strong for her.

The doctor adjusts himself in his chair. "It is still early enough in your pregnancy. You are within your rights to have an abortion."

Annette collects her composure. Her words reassure me of her endurance and ignite hope, "Abortion is not an option. If my child only has nine months to live, then it will be a happy nine months. We will let God decide his or her fate once born."

Our car is parked on the top deck of the parking garage. Exiting the building the air is cold, but the sun bright and the sky crystal blue. We pause before we enter the car. Annette looks at me and smiles. "We'll get through this. We must remain positive and happy for the sake of our child."

Chapter Two

Understanding

Understanding can overcome any situation, however mysterious or insurmountable it may appear to be.

Norman Vincent Peale

John Paul with his favorite girls from Outback

Fall 1998

The soft voice pierces the darkness. "Mom! Dad!" My feet hit the floor at the sound of his call. My heart beat intensifies. I am anxious, especially when he calls out in the middle of the night.

In the room I find my son sitting up in the middle of his bed. His hands rub his tired eyes, his disheveled hair protrudes awkwardly. I switch on the light and take a seat next to him on the bed.

"Are you okay, John Paul?"

He shakes his head yes, part of my anxiety diminishes.

"What's wrong?" I ask placing my arm around him.

"The wicked witch," His voice quivers with fear.

My embrace tightens around his small frame. "You know there is no such thing as the wicked witch. The Wizard of Oz is just a movie."

"But she's real in my dream."

"I know she seems real, but it is just make believe."

Slowly I lay him down and snuggle up beside him. He turns toward me.

"Daddy, next time I'll throw a bucket of water on her. That'll make her go away."

Understanding can be simple and it can be complex. John Paul's recurring nightmare will haunt him until he develops an understanding that the wicked witch is nothing more than a movie character. This notion is simple for adults to comprehend because of the ability to distinguish between real and make believe. However, even adults encounter obstacles in which understanding is void.

There have been numerous times when understanding has escaped me, starting with the shattering news of the diagnosis. My life, fortunately up to that point, had been uncomplicated. Sure there were obstacles, the South African Military demanded two years of mandatory military service at the age of eighteen. I resented giving the military two years of my life, but looking back my service infused a greater discipline. Plus the information provided to me as a Physical Training Instructor proved to be invaluable since John Paul's birth. After completing my duty I ventured alone to the states on a tennis scholarship. Both were trying times, but neither one a life-altering roadblock. That is something I never experienced until now. Each morning I wake with the same sick feeling in the pit of my stomach. How I desperately wish this was a nightmare I could wake from, but it isn't.

Winter 1994

The University of North Carolina is only a hour drive from our home. The teaching hospital, known for its cutting-edge medical technology, is where Annette and I choose to receive a second opinion on our unborn child's diagnosis.

I pull into the parking lot. Everywhere I look there are buildings. I locate the number and find a parking space nearby. Annette and I get out and start our expedition. Expedition may sound like a strange term to use, but for us this is an expedition. A journey we embark upon in order to gain understanding on the path before us.

The sunlight breaks through the clouds, but fails to offer warmth to the chilly day. At the entrance, hesitation sets in. I clutch Annette's hand a little tighter. The automatic doors shut behind me. I notice I am colder inside the building than outside. I look at Annette, she has on ivory leggings and an oversized black and red sweater her brother and sister gave her for Christmas. Even though worry is in every thread of her being, nature's natural maternal glow radiates from her. I'm sure her emotions are at a boiling point. Dealing with all the doctors and carrying a baby with an uncertain outcome has to be overwhelming. She amazes me. Each day my love for her deepens. Some people are a perfect fit, supposed to be together; I believe Annette and I were destined to be together. God had His plan. How else can it be described? It's ironic, our hometowns are on two different continents, mine below the equator. Annette, a senior, attended summer school because she needed a few extra credits to graduate. I had just started at the University in January and couldn't afford to go home so I worked on campus for the summer. You never know where love will find you. It found me in the cafeteria, of all places, on the first day of summer school. From that first meeting, there have been hurdles. We're total opposites. I'm constantly on the go, getting things done. Annette is a laid back mountain girl. She's into country music, I'm into eighties. The biggest difference is our background. The ocean not only separates our homes but also highlights the vast cultural diversities. After only dating a few weeks, I remember talking outside the gym at our university and telling her I didn't think this would work. I wasn't trying to be mean, but I didn't want to cause complications. She didn't give up.

"Things will work out. Think positive!"

We persevered, hurdles were cleared. We united as one and started a life together, but no hurdle is greater than the one we now face.

Walking the UNC Hospital hallways, everything looks the same. The décor, designed to emit a comforting feeling, transmits the opposite for me. As we enter the doctor's office I sign in and wait to be called. Time passes like a snail. Finally, we enter a similar room like the one at Wake Forest. We know the procedure, Annette lays on the table, I sit by her side and together we wait.

My mind plays this hopeful scenario. *Annette and I watch the UNC-Chapel Hill doctor complete the ultrasound. A smile eases across his face as he informs us that the scan shows no abnormalities. The original diagnosis had been a mistake.*

The visualization ceases as the doctor enters, introduces himself and commences the scan. I wait and watch for the smile to overcome the doctor's face. It never materializes. Instead his words are a carbon copy of Dr. Vegas's.

The previous optimism that entered after leaving Dr. Vega's office in Winston-Salem depletes. Two doctors from high-caliber hospitals have recited the same verdict. Reality settles in. The cloud of gloom seems destined to hover above.

In the days that follow the visit, a million questions race through my mind, but two that repeat over and over is how and why? I see Annette doing the same thing. She constantly questions herself. "Maybe I am to blame? Maybe I shouldn't have taken that Tylenol or what about that cough drop I had?" I tell her nothing she did caused this horrible situation. But my words do not ease her worry, nothing will. We are both suspended in the spiraling web of how and why.

It seems everywhere I turn there are visions of a happy family with a healthy, happy baby. It is apparent on the television, at the mall, at the grocery store and at church. Annette notices it too. This is supposed to be a happy time, the key word being *supposed*.

After Mass one Saturday night we decide to speak to Father Joe. We wait for him in a small room behind the sanctuary. Father Joe, an upbeat, positive man enters. We explain the news about our baby. In his heavy Irish brogue he replies to our news, "Leave your worries at the altar. Let God help you through."

Then I watch as he takes Annette's hands in his. "Let the light shine in. Wherever you are, open the curtains raise the blinds and get plenty of sunlight. Light is good for the soul and for healing."

Our families and friends unite around us, building a fortress of support. Through their love and prayers encouragement begins to emerge. The more we share our diagnosis with friends and acquaintances, the more lighted our path becomes and understanding is gained.

Glimmers of hope begin to spark.

Chapter Three

Signs

I need a sign to let me know you're here.

Train–Calling All Angels

John Paul with his bumble bee helmet

Traveling 1998

John Paul has a definitely witty sense of humor. I never will forget that after complications from surgery Annette and I made him wear a bright yellow helmet that had bumble bees all over it. The only time he took it off was at bedtime or when he was sitting in his car seat. One day we were traveling. John Paul was sitting in the back seat, his helmet off, watching a DVD. I was tried, so I pulled over and Annette got in the driver's seat while I dozed off. Annette said she had only been driving about ten minutes when she looked in the rearview mirror to check on John Paul. She could not contain her laughter. John Paul, seeing his mother in the driver's seat, reached to the other seat, got his helmet and secured it tightly on his head.

Spring 1994
From Annette:

My car hugs the curves of the two-lane road. I am on my way for a checkup. A few months have passed since the news, I try and remain positive. Time will not heal the wound. How can it as I watch my stomach grow? My baby's security is within me. I am in my sixth month. The clock ticks too quick. Only three to go until the unknown and uncertainty hits. I try not to think about the due date. I'm frightened it may be the end. This thought sends my hormones into overdrive. My hands cling to the steering wheel. I try to remain positive for the baby's sake, but sometimes I throw myself a pity party. Tears stream down my face. I turn up the radio. Suddenly a song comes on and changes my entire demeanor. I listen to the words, they speak to me.

I rub my stomach. "This is our song." I sing as loud as I can.

I can see clearly now the rain is gone. I can see all obstacles in my way.

Gone are the dark clouds that had me blind. It's gonna be a bright, bright sun shiny day.

I know this is a sign, it's hard to explain, but I feel a certain peace, a contentment that we will persevere.

There has been a bit of apprehension toward my doctor, Dr. Donner, due to the way he conveyed the news. Also, his feelings on the outcome of the pregnancy does not help my morale. I enter the office and focus on the good vibration received from hearing the song.

Being the only OBGYN in town, the office is always busy; today is no exception. I walk to the window, sign in and take a seat on the couch in front of the television. The receptionist calls me back to the window.

"I want to let you know that Dr. Donner is in emergency surgery; Dr. Keever will see you today."

I tell her that is fine and take a seat back on the couch and wait. My eyes focus on the large television playing continuous commercials on being healthy. I stare at the screen, but my mind wanders. I think about seeing a new doctor. I have seen Dr. Keever at church, but I have never had an office visit with him. A child running across the waiting room breaks my concentration. I look at my watch, it is taking longer than normal. I flip through magazines and occupy myself until finally my name is called.

In the exam room I am alone, which is a rarity these days. This solitude gives me time to think. Derek and I both come from very devout Christian backgrounds. I was raised a Baptist, my dad a Baptist minister; the aspect of God, faith and church was the foundation of my existence. Derek had that same foundation through his Catholic faith; his family incorporated God, faith, church and prayer in their daily lives. We merged as one united in our belief in God and faith. It is very easy and simple to live by faith when times are good, but troubling times often puts faith to the test. This is our test, our cross. I realize there are choices: lay low and hope everything works out or take control of the situation. I think about my faith, the prayers of family and friends, people of all denominations uniting in praying for our unborn child. I know all these things fused together will sustain us. I think about the song of the radio, how it came on at the right moment. My mom always says, "No one knows what tomorrow holds, but we know who holds it." No doctor can dictate the future of my child. Only the One above has control of the situation and I am placing my trust in Him. My job is to continue to pray, continue to ask others for their prayers and make sure the remainder of my pregnancy is healthy and positive. Fear must be turned into perseverance.

Dr. Keever enters the room, tall, lanky and full of life.

"Hello Miss Annette," He says in a slow southern Alabama drawl.

"Hello." It seems odd seeing him at church and now seeing him in this capacity, but his demeanor has a settling effect.

"So, how are things going?" He takes a seat on the rolling stool and glances at my chart.

"Fine." My answer is a traditional southern response, no matter what the ailment or the state of mind at the time of the question, fine is the reply.

"Now I know there is a lot going on in your life. Are you sure you are really fine?"

I smile. "Trying to be."

He pushes a button, the nurse enters, he conducts the routine exam. Then does something out of the ordinary from Dr. Donner, he talks. Not just about my feelings and apprehensions, but the possible outcome of my pregnancy. He is not bleak or pessimistic, he offers hope and encouragement with stories of past experiences.

"I always think it helps to hear of others who have overcome obstacles. Theirs may not be the same, but similar." He pauses before continuing on. "You've made your decision to deliver this baby, and I applaud you. Remember to cherish the time you have with your child, whether it be a day, five years or fifty years. Every day is a blessing. Stay positive!"

On the way out of the office I realize it is imperative that I surround myself and my unborn child with positive reinforcements. So, before I leave I inform the receptionist that I prefer Dr. Keever to be my physician from now on.

As I turn down the street toward home, I am surprised to see Derek's car in the driveway at this time of day, but I'm happy he is home. I enter the house with a smile on my face.

"That's nice to see," Derek says.

"What?" I ask giving him a hug as I sit down beside him.

"A smile. Looks like you had a good visit."

"Actually I did, but it wasn't with Dr. Donner. He wasn't in today. I saw Dr. Keever."

"He goes to our church, doesn't he?"

"Yes, and you know what? He's the first doctor who didn't question our decision to carry the baby to term. More importantly, he said there is always hope. Can you believe it? Finally a doctor who doesn't dwell on the negative, but instead introduces positive reinforcement."

Derek pulls me close and kisses my forehead. "I am happy to see the sparkle of hope in your eyes. Not only that, but I see that positive persuasion I fell in love with years ago."

Chapter Four

Hope

Hope is the thing with feathers— That perches in the soul— And sings the tune without the words— And never stops—at all.

Emily Dickenson

John Paul at the Honda Classic

March 2009

Annette received a call late Wednesday afternoon from a gentleman in charge of the standard bearers for the Honda Classic Golf Tournament. He explained that John Paul's golf coach had given

evening with a meal, feasting on fish and chips. Afterward we take our seats at an outdoor concert venue and listen to Gary Morris sing "Wind Beneath My Wings" and other hits. After the concert, we decide to head to Krispy Kreme, Annette's favorite. By the time we arrive it is nearly midnight, but that doesn't stop us, Annette has a craving. She orders half a dozen doughnuts for herself and an ice cold coke. We laugh at how quickly she devours the hot doughnuts.

We arrive home a little after twelve thirty, and both go straight to bed.

From Annette:

By two in the morning I am tossing and turning. I figure too many doughnuts. I slowly get out of bed, trying not to wake Derek. I go into the family room, turn on the television and watch cheerleading competitions. I can not get comfortable. No matter what I do, sit, stand, lay, I feel uneasy. I pace the floor most of the night. Finally, at about six o'clock I go to the bathroom, my water breaks. For a minute I am in shock. This is it!

"Derek!" I call.

At the sound of my voice his feet hit the floor, and he is at the bathroom door in two seconds flat.

"I think it's time." I look at Derek who has just been waken from a deep sleep. Suddenly his eyes pop open. "Can you call my mom?"

He bolts out the bathroom and dials my mom. My family lives next door so she was by my side in a matter of minutes. I watch Derek and my mom whirl around each other like two mini tornadoes, trying to gather my things. I ask Derek to put my shoes on. He attempts to do so, but he is so fidgety I finally tell him I will do it. My mom kneels beside me, I kiss her on the cheek, I see the tears in her eyes, and she knows how worried and anxious I am.

"Everything will be fine," she tells me with great conviction and I believe her, she is my rock.

Derek helps me up and places his arm around my waist. Slowly we walk to the car. Once in the car everything seems surreal. Is this it? Is it really time? What is going to happen now? *Dear God help me, help Derek, but more importantly help our baby.*

The hazard lights blink rapidly, cars move too slowly for Derek. He weaves in and out of the Saturday morning farmer and flea market traffic.

County Memorial, in Winston-Salem, is where I go to have our child. I can not go to my local hospital; they are not equipped to handle my baby. County is in close proximity to North Carolina Hospital, home of Bentley's Children's Hospital, one of the best neo-natal facilities in the state.

Derek helps me into the hospital. Within minutes I am in a wheelchair on the way to my room. Derek and I toured the maternity floor early in my pregnancy, but I didn't remember the rooms being as large as mine. It doesn't feel like a hospital room, it is more comforting. Everything is decorated in light wood with pink wallpaper, which makes me wonder if they know something I don't. For thirty minutes or more nurses come in and out. One nurse remains by my side making sure I am comfortable. She tells me she will be with me at all times. If I need anything I must let her know. I do not know what I need. I do not know what I am supposed to be feeling. One thing I do know is that the pain is starting to intensify.

"How much longer?" I ask my nurse.

"Depends, first time deliveries can be long and drawn out. The doctor should be in soon. He is finishing up a delivery."

Derek tries his best to make me comfortable, staying by my side, holding my hand. Petrified is the only word that describes how I feel. My baby is ready to enter this world with a fate unknown. Anticipation and anxiety mingle together and filter from me to Derek to our families waiting outside my door. Everyone is here except my mom, who has stayed home to care for my brother and sister. She's not here, but she has already started manning the phone, calling friends and family to start the pray chain.

have known the diagnosis for nine months her words infuse reality, and instigate life and death decisions. She carefully discusses the options for management. The information overwhelms me. My approval must be given before a procedure can take place, and the decision that can be life-altering must be made instantly. At this point, she tells me John Paul will need to be tube fed and intubated (place on a respirator), and asks if I will consent to this procedures. Terms I have never heard of come at me; all I know is if it will help save my son's life, then I want it done.

I want John Paul baptized. I request a priest, but I am unsure when he will be able to come. I can't wait, but I do not have holy water. I walk over to the nurse's station and ask for a cup of water, it isn't holy, but I know Jesus will bless the ordinary water. Back at John Paul's bedside I pray silently. When I open my eyes I dip my thumb in the water. Slowly and carefully I place my thumb on his forehead and bless him with the sign of the cross, in the name of the Father, the Son and the Holy Spirit. My eyes moisten at the intimate moment I share with my son. For an instance life is still and peaceful.

The next morning my parents and I go to see John Paul during visiting hours. While infants are in NICU, parents and immediate relatives are only allowed to visit during certain hours. Today, as I enter, my stomach churns. John Paul is intubated. He lays flat on his back, his arms and legs sprawled apart. When the doctor told me they may have to intubate him, I really did not know what that meant, only it would help him breathe. A large plastic blue tube protrudes out of his mouth. The tube connects to a machine lit up with lights and knobs, a ventilator. The noise from the ventilator reminds me of being in a wind tunnel. Next I notice a tube coming out of his nose. Part of the tube is taped to his cheek. My eyes follow the tube and find it hooked to a small machine on a chrome pole. A bag hangs from the top of the pole, cream-colored liquid flows through the tube.

"What's that?" I ask the nurse.

"That is John Paul's food. He is being tube fed in order to receive nutrition."

How I wish someone could have prepared me for this vision. Told me what to expect, not just use terms that are incomprehensible to the average person. Explaining the procedures and how my son will look and what is to be expected could have reduced some anxiety.

My mom, dad and I stand by John Paul, not much is said. We offer up prayers in the silence of our hearts. Our thoughts are interrupted by a doctor who introduces himself, Dr. Bland. I notice the accent right away, South African. I can't believe it, Dr. Bland is from my homeland. The kinship briefly eases my inner tension. He explains the options for John Paul briefly. He states that a surgical procedure may help John Paul. At those words I am flabbergasted. Never once in all the doctor visits has surgery ever been mentioned. We were told of two options, do nothing or be placed on the list for a heart transplant. The transplant would be a long shot. We would be required to move to California and wait. It was made clear that the severity of his condition may not provide him enough time for a heart to be found. But now, surgery is an option. I can't believe it. Annette and I have always stated, if surgery could correct or help his condition, then we would proceed.

"I'll set up an appointment for tomorrow June sixth at two o'clock. You will meet with Dr. Harmon, Chief of Cardiothoracic Surgery. Dr. Penski and I will also be in attendance. Dr. Harmon will be able to answer any questions you may have about John Paul's options."

My adrenaline is pumping, I can't wait to get back to the hospital and tell Annette that there may be a surgical procedure to help John Paul. Finally there is hope, no matter how minuet at least there is a ray shinning down.

Chapter Five

Counsel

The counsel of God is, as it were, his deliberation over the best manner of accomplishing anything already approved by the understanding and the will.

William Ames

John Paul and Jane Seymour

Spring 2008

I watch John Paul run to the car. I roll down the window.

"Can I play one more song on the piano for Grandma and mom?"

"Sure," I shout back and watch him dash back into his grand-parents' house.

After a few minutes he and Annette come to the car. Annette carries the Beatles CD, One, which I purchased for John Paul a few weeks ago. He takes piano and guitar and loves to try to play along with the Beatles and McCartney.

"Tell dad how good I played mom," his voice sounds from the back seat.

Annette looks in my direction. "He played great, you should've heard him."

"What song did you play?" I ask, knowing for certain it was Let it Be. I had heard his small hands strum the strings and attempt to dazzle the keyboard for weeks trying to play the song.

"Put the CD in and turn it to number twenty-six and you will hear my song."

I insert the CD.

"When I find myself in times of trouble Mother Mary comes to me speaking words of wisdom let it be," John Paul's voice echoes over McCartney's.

At that moment it hits me, what a compelling song. For the past thirteen years I have sought counsel not only from Mother Mary, but also her Son and those who surround me. How ironic that John Paul, for over a month, has been playing the title for me. Let It Be... He had his guitar teacher write down the notes so he could learn. He has been at the piano daily trying to pick up the tune by ear. I just didn't take notice.

I play the sound again and listen to the lyrics. Let It Be...

June 1994

Insecurity breeds fear and my anxiety is in overload. I keep repeating in my mind the words Dr. Bland said. "There may be a surgical procedure to help John Paul." How wonderful that will be, but what does this surgery entail. What will be the outcome? He did not elaborate, so Annette and I have to wait twenty-four hours to find out. Twenty-four hours to contemplate the unknown. I sit at the foot of Annette's hospital bed. We are in deep conversation. We realize the importance of the meeting tomorrow with the surgeon; time is of the essence and a decision will have to be made promptly. I think back, as a child I could not wait until I became old enough to make my own decisions, but now the decision made will determine fate, the fate of my son. In my heart I know what Annette and I want, but this isn't just about our wants. The discussion is interrupted by a gentle knock on the door.

"Come in," I say turning to face the door.

In walks a priest. I believe God sends people into our lives for a reason, and He sent this priest to us. After a few minutes of small talk we begin to tell the priest of John Paul's situation and our dilemma.

The words spoke by the priest were an inspiration to me that day in June of 1994 and are still an inspiration to this day:

You've done your part. You've brought John Paul into the world. Now let John Paul show you what he can do.

With these words we receive our counsel.

It's the first time Annette has been able to see John Paul since he was hurriedly whisked away after birth. To her, the birth is dreamlike, she hasn't been able to confirm John Paul's existence. I have told her all about his unruly jet black hair, long dark lashes, full pink lips and cute nose, and how the nurses have already nicknamed him Ringo because of his Beatle connection name, John Paul George. But only through seeing will validation set in.

"It's important for you to hold John Paul and bond with him," I tell her as we walk down the hall of the hospital. "Dr. Bland encouraged me to make sure you do that." She doesn't respond, she hasn't said much since we got out of the car.

"Are you okay?"

She shakes her head and tries to smile, but I can sense the worry. I can not fathom what she feels, not only emotionally, but physically. I am worried about her, she withholds her emotions.

I would not push the bonding issue, but Dr. Bland has been persistent in the importance so I try and convey this to Annette in baby steps.

We both pause at the entrance of NICU. I take her hand in mine, I've tried to prepare her for what she is about to see. Her grip tightens. I open the door we walk hand in hand. I watch her eyes scan from one crib to the next.

"This is so sad, look at all these babies." Her eyes fill with fear. "I don't know if I can handle this."

I gently tug her hand and pull her to John Paul's crib. Her grip releases, she walks over and stands beside him. Her trembling hand carefully caresses his face. Her eyes lock with mine.

"He's beautiful." Tears stream down her face, I place my arm tightly around her.

"Would you like to hold him?" The nurse asks.

Her eyes remain on John Paul. "There's so many tubes and everything."

"Honey, that's no problem," the nurse says.

Annette hesitates. "Maybe tomorrow."

The nurse explains all the tubes and machines to Annette, she tries to focus on the words, but she is consumed by our son. Afterwards the nurse leaves to administer to another patient. We stand by the bed together, one on each side of John Paul.

I glance at Annette, and again ask, "Are you okay?"

"This is overpowering, all the machines and everything. I know you tried to prepare me, but seeing John Paul in this condition is just…" She stops short of finishing the sentence, I notice her bottom lip quivering, unable to contain herself any longer she breaks down in my arms. Months of anxiety and pressure release. I am not sure how long we stand in entwined; finally Annette pulls away, wipes her eyes and moves closer to John Paul. The tips of her fingers stroke his hair. "Do you think he can hear us?"

"I know he feels our presence, and yes I think he can hear us. That's why it's very important we talk to him, touch him, kiss him, tell him we love him, make sure he feels our love."

The nurse interrupts our conversation to inform us that the surgeon is waiting in the conference room down the hall. I squeeze John Paul's hand and Annette kisses him on the forehead before we leave.

Outside of NICU we pause.

"Isn't it amazing? That's our son in there," Annette says beaming.

"Are you sure you didn't want to hold him?"

"No. It seems everyone is pushing the subject of bonding, it makes me uncomfortable. It's like the doctors and nurses want me to bond because they do not expect John Paul to live and our bonding needs to take place before it's too late." She stops in the hallway and looks directly into my eyes. "I don't know, maybe I am just scared."

I can't argue with her feelings, so I remain silent.

The conference room is slightly lighted by a few windows along the wall. I recognize Dr. Penski and Dr. Bland who are seated on opposite sides of the table. The surgeon stands as we enter.

"Hello, I am Dr. Harmon, Chief of Cardiothorastic Surgery." He extends his hand to meet mine.

"Nice to meet you, I am Derek George and this is my wife, Annette." We take a seat across the table from the doctor.

Dr. Harmon, very personable, in his mid fifties, fair hair and blue eyes begins the conversation with optimistic news.

"I examined your son and he is a good candidate for the Norwood Procedure."

I look at Annette and then back to Dr. Harmon. "What is the Norwood Procedure?"

The doctor explains a very complicated procedure simply enough for Annette and I to understand. In layman's terms, the goal of this completed procedure is to have the right side of the heart, which normally only pumps blood to the lungs, pump blood to the entire body. The Norwood is split into three different stages. The first stage, conducted a few days after birth, allows the right side of the heart to pump blood to the upper body. This stage is very important, it determines if the heart is strong enough to withstand the pressure of what it is being asked to do. The second stage re-routes the blood to the mid section of the body. This stage usually takes place during the first year after birth. The third and final stage takes the blood to the lower extremities completing the three stage procedure. This stage is usually completed during the third year. The Norwood is entirely experimental which is made crystal clear to me and Annette. Although Dr. Harmon has performed the Norwood Procedure before, the surgery has never been attempted at the North Carolina Hospital.

"I'll be perfectly honest, the odds are not good." Dr. Harmon leans across the table and shows a diagram of the heart. "One thing in John Paul's favor, the hole which allows blood flow is larger than normal therefore the surgery is better suited for him."

Questions swarm back and forth. Like a sponge I soak up every-thing the doctor says. This goes on for over a hour and a half; finally the doctors leave me and Annette alone in the conference room to contemplate all the information tossed at us. There is so much to process, but time is short, a decision must be made by morning.

With the profound words of the priest still fresh in our minds we make our decision and go back to NICU to visit John Paul. Dr. Harmon is at John Paul's bedside.

"He's a lovely child," Dr. Harmon says with an endearing smile on his face.

"Thank you," Annette says, she walks over and stands beside the doctor.

"We made our decision." The doctor glances from John Paul to me. "We have done our part now let John Paul show us what he can do."

Dr. Harmon nods.

Annette tugs at the doctor's arm. "Please take good care of him."

Chapter Six

Strength

You gain strength, courage, and confidence by every experience in which you really stop to look fear in the face. You are able to say to yourself, I lived through this horror. I can take the next thing that comes along.

Eleanor Roosevelt

John Paul showing off his Manchester United gear

June 2007

The condo is partially furnished so the slightest noise reverberates off the walls. I hear a swish of wind outside my door as John

Paul runs by, I gaze at the lighted alarm clock, 6:30 a.m. I didn't sleep well last night; however, that seems to happen every year around this time. It is as though my body psychologically reverts back and tenses, reliving events from years ago. *This is a happy time,* I remind myself, yet the mystical mind is hard to control.

Once again the swish breezes around outside my bedroom door and I hear a faint giddy giggle. Finally I muster enough willpower to get out of bed. I walk through the kitchen and look at the refrigerator. Annette has posted a handwritten birthday card in red, blue and green marker on the refrigerator, Happy 13th Birthday John Paul, We Love You! You are the Love of Our Lives! I look closer, John Paul has made his own notation, Mom and Dad I Love You Too!

I reach his bedroom door, peak in and watch for a few minutes, I feel a joy in my heart that is unexplainable. Thirteen years, and they said he wouldn't live past birth. How can I feel anything but joy?

"Happy birthday my son!" I push the door open, stretch out my arms and encompass him in a huge bear hug.

"Thanks daddy. Since today's my birthday, I get to do anything, and I mean anything I want. Right daddy?"

"Anything?"

His eyes sparkle and a mischievous grin spreads across his face. "Well, it is my birthday, I deserve it!"

I can't argue with that, considering all he has been through he does deserve it. Each passing year I am more amazed at the graces God has bestowed on my family. The fourth of June is a time of celebration and thanksgiving, but it is also a time of reflection. Everyday I think about all John Paul has endured, somehow on his birthday I relive all the events of his life in one day. This birthday is no different.

June 9, 1994

Today is excruciating, no other word describes how I feel. Annette and I stand by John Paul's crib; it is almost more than I can stand.

Every part of my body is trembling, I can't control it. This is the most important day of his young life. I can't bear to look at him, I am fearful it may be the last time I see him alive. I know I shouldn't think that way, but I can't help it. I just signed the consent forms, it is written in black and white, possible complication from the surgery is death. He has only been in my life for five days yet his impact on me is astronomical, I can't tolerate the thought of losing him. I look at Annette and sense she is dealing with the same thoughts.

"This is tough," her words are soft, almost a whisper. "He's going to be fine," she states, but her eyes question mine.

Although doubts flurry, I respond with conviction, "Absolutely, he's going to be fine." I have to believe my own words, nothing else in the world matters right now.

Only two family members are allowed in NICU at a time, but today the rules are bent for our family. The nurse allows both of our parents to stay with us until John Paul leaves for surgery. We gather around his crib, talk to him, tell him we love him, and to be strong, Jesus is with him. I feel a slight touch on my back. I turn and notice a nun in a cream-colored habit. She is very petite and appears to be in her early seventies.

"I'm Sister Eileen Dennis from St. Paul's."

"It's a pleasure to meet you Sister. My name is Derek and this is my wife Annette." I introduce our parents and she enters the circle we have formed around John Paul.

"What a beautiful boy. What's his name?"

"His name is John Paul, we named him after the Pope."

"That's lovely." She steps closer to John Paul, her crinkled hand slowly touches his head she leans down and whispers something in his ear. She stands by his side for a few minutes, her hand clasped around his arm, her eyes intently focused on my son.

"Who is John Paul's doctor?" She asks returning to my side.

"Dr. Harmon."

"He's a great doctor and a good Christian man. I have known him for a long time."

She must see the worry in my eyes because she gathers Annette and me closer to her and takes both of our hands into hers.

"Is John Paul your only child?"

"Yes Sister," we respond in unison.

"Ask Jesus to place John Paul's heart in His Sacred Heart and to place the surgeon's hands in His hands."

Talk about a Godsend, this pint-size lady is a full-size blessing, definitely a person God let enter my life for a reason.

Somberness enters as the surgical team arrives to take John Paul to surgery. Sister Dennis excuses herself and tells us she will see us later. Our parents each kiss John Paul and go to the waiting room. Annette and I remain; we watch the team dressed in green scrubs prepare to move John Paul. The nurse approaches,

"If you like, you may walk down to the O.R. with John Paul."

"We'd like that, thank you."

We follow our son down the corridor to a special elevator. Inside the elevator I notice my legs are like strings of spaghetti; I back up against the wall to sturdy myself. The doors open, Annette and I follow John Paul down a short hallway; ahead I see the entrance to the operating room. I begin to wonder if I will be able to keep my composure. The surgical team stops in front of the doors.

"This is as far as you can go," the one gentleman says reaching to press the automatic door opener.

I lean down, make the sign of the cross on John Paul's forehead and repeat Sister Dennis's words, "Please sweet Jesus, I place John Paul's heart in your sacred heart and please place the surgeon's hands in your sacred hands." I slowly kiss him and soak up his sweet newborn scent. I stand back, and Annette places her index finger inside John Paul's hand. I watch his grip tighten around his mother's finger. Tears well up in my eyes. Annette leans in and kisses his cheek. Reluctantly we step away, we watch him enter the doorway to the operating room, our eyes follow him until he is no longer visible. Annette and I slowly walk down the hallway, conversation is void; we are both too overwhelmed to speak.

The surgical waiting room on the first floor of the hospital is where we wait. The large windowless room is lined with chairs, a vending machine section and an information desk staffed with volunteers. Annette and I find our families and begin our long wait. The clock on the wall moves slower with every passing hour. I walk to the information desk for a status update each hour, but the answer is the same, still in surgery. I do not know what to do with myself.

Television, magazines, nothing occupies me. I do not feel like talking, I can not stay focused long enough to carry on a conversation. I pace, pray and contemplate. Finally, after ten hours a volunteer calls over the speaker, George family. Annette and I rush to her desk.

"Did you call George family?"

"Yes sir, John Paul George is out of surgery."

"Is he okay?" I ask.

"I'm sorry, that's all the information I have. The doctor will be in shortly."

A heavy weight lifts off my shoulders, at least John Paul is out of surgery, but doubt trickles in. *Sure he is out of surgery, but what if…* I think back to the day Annette had the sonogram, having to wait on the doctor for results. I know I am paranoid; I shake my head, clear my thoughts. Annette puts her arms around my waist and squeezes tightly.

We walk back, tell our family the news and sit momentarily in relief.

Annette's body jolts out of her chair. "There's Dr. Harmon."

I stand up beside her, frozen, unable to move. Dr. Harmon is in green scrubs, and green Birkenstock clogs. He is still wearing his surgical cap and his mask is loosely draped around his neck. I try to analyze the doctor's face as he walks toward us, all I see is depletion. He meets us with weak smile.

"The surgery went well, John Paul is in recovery."

Annette's reflexes bounce her in my arms. Before I know it she is hugging Dr. Harmon and thanking him profusely. I do the manly thing, a firm handshake, but emotions soar, so I hug Dr. Harmon as well. He doesn't seem to mind, in his eyes I see the same thankfulness we are feeling.

"The next forty-eight hours will be crucial. He should be up in 5A, which is the intensive care unit, in an hour and a half. Go get something to eat and I will see you up there later."

"Thank you doctor, thank you so much."

Annette repeats the same words, we do not know what to do with ourselves, we are ecstatic. We share the news with our family and count our blessings. One hurdle cleared! Finally I am able to breathe, I exhale and resolve myself to focus on John Paul's recovery.

I can not remember the last time Annette and I had something to eat and with the good news her appetite ignites.

"Let's go to the cafeteria and get something to eat," she says tugging at my arm.

Since John Paul's birth, stress consumes her desire for food, so with delight I watch her devour a cheeseburger and French fries. I do not want to waste much time; as soon as we eat Annette and I go up to the fifth floor and wait in the small ICU waiting area. As the day turns to evening I find myself ending the day the same way I started it, waiting. Forty-five minutes later the nurse calls Annette and I to ICU.

ICU on the fifth floor is for adult heart patients, it is very rare for a newborn to be in the unit. Annette and I enter, the unit is full and the sound of machines stationed by each bed is intense. From the doorway I see his crib in the middle of the floor directly in front of the nurse station. I notice the same machines from NICU surround him, but as I inch closer my heart drops. Not anything could have prepared me for the image before me. *Dear God, is this the same baby?* If it wasn't for his hair I would not have recognized my son. It is difficult for me to describe the vision. His face is like a balloon, his eyes are swollen shut, just the tip end of his long lashes are visible, his skin is black and blue. He is naked, except for a diaper. In the middle of John Paul's tiny chest is an incision smothered with Betadine, it stretches the length of his chest. At this moment I realize this incision will turn into a scar, a daily reminder of my son's plight. How will I explain the scar to him, when the time comes?

Visiting hours ended long ago, but the doctors allow Annette and I to remain a few minutes longer with our son. We both stand beside the crib in disbelief, unsure what to do, how to act. Sister Dennis arrives and joins us, together we silently pray for his recovery. The nurse in charge of John Paul gives Annette a sheet of paper with the visiting hours schedule and a phone number to call for updates. We are told the unit strictly adheres to the times for the well-being of the patients.

It is time to go, I can't bear to leave, but we will not be allowed back in until ten the next morning and the nurse assures us she will call if there is any change. I kiss John Paul on the top of his head and start toward the door, I struggle to leave, I look back repeatedly before I finally exit through the automatic doors.

A good night's sleep, I do not know what that is. My last peaceful night's sleep occurred on June 3rd 1994, since then my sleep is restless, too many constant worries. I am totally exhausted from worry, but unable to sleep. Annette is the same way; she calls the hospital throughout the night for updates. A ray of sun pierces through the window, with it is the hope of a new day. Every day is a carbon copy of the previous. Annette and I arrive at the hospital early and wait for visiting hours to commence. Fifteen minutes, that's the time allotted. We remain at the hospital throughout the day waiting for the next fifteen minutes. At night, we arrive home around nine; during intermittent sleep Annette phones for updates on John Paul. After a couple of days we stop going home, we stay at the hospital around the clock.

The doctors explained the complexity of the surgery during our conference, but my naivety failed to consider the obstacles of recovery and aftercare. The first eight days bumps have occurred, but nothing major. On June 16th the doctor states that John Paul is ready to be extubated. Extubation means his breathing tube will be removed, a machine will no longer sustain his life. I am excited, the doctors feel he is ready to breathe on his own, a major accomplishment. The breathing tube is removed around noon; however complications set in, and by two o'clock John Paul is reintubated. The excitement from earlier flutters, John Paul seems to be on a downhill spiral.

My first Father's Day, June 19th starts off on a good note, John Paul is stable. That is the best news, can't think of a better gift, but by noon my emotions dip south. John Paul has taken a turn for the worse. His platelet and white count have decreased, as well as his blood sugar. Annette and I are at his bedside.

"I have contacted Dr. Shaw; there is a possibility that John Paul's bowel is dying," Dr. Harmon explains in response to John Paul's abdomen x-ray and abnormal blood work.

Dr. Harmon advises that Dr. Shaw will do an exploratory surgery. If the bowel is dead it will be removed.

I am concerned. John Paul has just had open heart surgery a few days ago and now this. What if his heart is not able to withstand the pressure of a surgery? Dr. Harmon assures me there is no other alternative. The surgery has to be done.

I sign the consent form and within minutes Annette and I watch as John Paul is wheeled away. Doctors and nurses surround his crib. The ventilator that breathes for him is still in ICU, a nurse manually bags John Paul in place of the ventilator and with every step the others monitor his vitals.

My spirit sinks. *This can't be my first and last Father's Day rolled into one!*

Once again Annette and I take a seat in the surgical waiting room. I notice there is no volunteer stationed at the desk and the seats are plentiful on this late Sunday afternoon. Mentally drained, words fail me. All I have the strength to do is sit and tightly hold Annette's hand. I watch the clock on the wall and wonder if the wait will be as long as the other day. Around six o'clock I see Dr. Shaw walk into the waiting room. The news is good. John Paul's bowel is fine and he is back in ICU. Cultures from his central lines grew E. Coli and several other staph infections. Antibiotics are started to try to clear the severe infection.

Back in ICU I stand by the crib and can not help but notice where another scar will be. Right where his vertical incision from the open heart surgery ends begins the horizontal incision from the stomach surgery. Scars are superficial, I just thank God for blessing me this Father's Day with my beautiful son.

June 29, 1994

The uncertainty continues. John Paul is going back into the operating room to make adjustments to the Norwood Procedure conducted on June the 4th. Dr. Harmon plans to revise the shunt between the pulmonary arteries and the aorta. This is necessary because John Paul has developed pulmonary hypertension. This is when tiny arteries in the lungs become narrow or blocked. This causes increased resistance to the flow of blood in the lungs, which in turn raises pressure within the pulmonary arteries. As the pressure builds, the heart's lower right chamber (right ventricle) must work harder to pump blood through the lungs, eventually causing the heart muscle to weaken and sometimes to fail completely. The consensus of the doctors: the shunt is too small and needs to widen to allow proper blood flow.

Again, Annette and I wait... The revision is successful but I can not help but wonder what will come next.

My emotions are like a rubber ball bouncing from wall to wall. Annette is no better than me. Her state of mind concerns me. She hardly eats; the last time she had a full meal was June 9th. Her diet consists of coke, crackers and a candy bar every now and then. Her face is hollow I do not know how much more she can take.

Worry hangs over my head constantly; it is the monkey who will not get off my back. Even on days when everything seems to be operating smoothly, there is that constant worry of what will go wrong next. I thought after the first surgery John Paul was on the road to recovery. Then Father's Day spiked anxiety and doubt with the stomach surgery, and the serious staph infection. And now the shunt… Every day is a challenge to my faith.

From Annette:

I am basically on auto-pilot, that's the best way to describe my demeanor at this stage. My son has had to clear so many hurdles, I'm in awe at all the miracles which have been gifted to John Paul from above in his short life. I am grateful that the doctors were able to revise his shunt and pray this is the last obstacle.

Derek and I stand by John Paul's crib where we have been since he returned from surgery. His vitals are good and we are overwhelmed with relief. It's late and Dr. Renar encourages us to go home and get a good night's sleep. We are reluctant; we do not want to leave John Paul. However, she sees the stress revealing itself on our weary faces and tells us we should go get some much-needed rest in order to be refreshed when John Paul wakes up. Neither of us intend to leave but her logical words persuade us so we kiss John Paul and hesitantly depart.

Once home, I call the nurses station and with confirmation that John Paul is still doing fine and then go to bed. Around midnight a phone call summonds us to the hospital; John Paul has taken a turn for the worse. Although I've only been a mother for a few days I wished I had listened to my maternal intuition and stayed at the hospital.

Everything is a blur until I enter the intensive care unit. At that point the images are vivid and crystal clear; John Paul is in dire straits. A team of doctors and nurses are hovering over my son's crib tactically contemplating what to do. The anxiety etched upon Dr. Renar's face as she approaches causes my knees to buckle. She explains that John Paul's saturations are dropping dangerously low and his brain and lungs are being starved for air. The trauma is placing extreme pressure on his already frail heart. As a last resort John Paul is going to be placed on a jet ventilator to try to revive his oxygen levels. She adds that the prognosis is not good and the chance of survival is very slim to none.

Although we do not want to leave, Derek and I are asked to wait in the waiting room. I watch Derek shift through the doctors and nurses until he is beside John Paul's crib. He leans down and whispers something into our son's ear, kisses him, then together we exit intensive care and enter the waiting room.

We are alone in the small room. Our hands are entwined but conversation is void as Derek's head is bowed. For no particular reason my eyes are focused on the door and the bare hallway outside as I fervently pray for my son.

Out of nowhere he appears. The first thing which beckons my gaze are his brilliant vibrant blue gentle eyes. They lasso my attention. He pulls a dull gray trashcan up beside him as he stops at the doorway. His ebony skin is etched with numerous wrinkles and his clothes are worn. Bending down he rubs his knee as his tender eyes focus on Derek's lowered head and defeated appearance.

"My knee is killing me; I need to take a seat for a few minutes," he says.

His eyes never advert from my husband, and I watch without saying a word as he sits down in the chair next to Derek. With his head still bowed, Derek has not taken notice of the gentleman.

The old man proceeds to rub both knees and continues to speak, "Family's real important."

It's hard to describe, but the tone of his voice is comforting, and I am captivated. When Derek hears the gentleman's word he responds without looking up. I observe as the man removes his hand from his knee and places it on Derek's leg. His touch brings Derek's gaze upward to meet his. I witness the effect.

The conversation proceeds:

"My son, you have a child in there."

It isn't a question but rather a statement, but Derek answers, "Yes, but it doesn't look good."

With his hand still on Derek's leg he continues, "Don't worry everything is going to be fine." His words are precise and spoken in a tender and loving manner. I am in awe and still processing the words of this kind elderly man when a nurse rushes to the doorway calling us back to intensive care.

Upon entering Derek and I spot Dr. Renar standing in the middle of the room. Gone is the anxiety and despair which earlier captured and etched her face. The hopelessness is replaced with a bright illuminated smile.

Derek asks, "What happened?"

She informs us that John Paul's staturations shot back up and his functions were returning to normal. She proceeds to proclaim this miracle could have only come from one place, and she shot her hands upward to heaven.

Derek searches for the elderly man but is unable to find him. We never saw him again. The warm sensation which penetrated Derek's leg at the man's touch is still unfathomable to this day. Both of us will never forget the beauty and serenity of his eyes and the validity of his words.

The presence of God is like air, it surrounds us…

Going Home

I can see clearly now the rain is gone

It has been nearly two months since John Paul ventured into the world. It goes without saying that his life thus far has been complicated, but he is not alone. I am sitting beside his crib in NICU taking note of the surroundings, small helpless beings, some the size of my hand, whose source of life comes from machines. There have been dark days when a child's fight is long enough. I watch in agony as torment filters through the family; my heart cannot bear to see the pain. There are also the joyful times when a family finally gets to take their son or daughter home.

The outside world is a distant place. I can honestly say for fifty plus days nothing that is going on beyond the doors of NICU matters to me. My only concern is my son. Today is a big day, the day I have been praying for. John Paul is coming home.

Thrill and anxiety mold into one. I am happy to take my son home; however, gone will be the security of having a doctor or nurse at my fingertips. Karen, John Paul's nurse from NICU will be able to visit our home twice a week to help with any needs or concerns.

The last few days have been a crash course in home health care for John Paul. Annette and I have both been retrained and certified in CPR. We have been shown how to administer his medications and insert his feeding tube. This without a doubt is the most difficult. In order to receive nutrition a small tube must be inserted into John Paul's nose. The tube is measured, then must be slowly pushed down into his stomach. Proper placement is vital. In the hospital each insertion is checked by x-ray. Unfortunately, at home a stethoscope will be used to check placement. Today is the test to verify if I am able to complete the insertion. Slowly I insert the tube. I take the stethoscope and place it on John Paul's stomach. With a syringe I push air through the tube and listen for the specific sound that lets me know that the placement is correct. I nod my head to the nurse that the placement is correct; she verifies with a swish of air through the tube. She smiles and pats me on the back. "Good job."

In order to be released both parents must be able to complete the insertion procedures. Annette is next. She is nervous. Her hands tremble; carefully she inserts the tube and continues the steps. "I think I got it!" She smiles taking the stethoscope out of her ears. The nurse verifies and congratulates her on a job well done.

Annette and I begin to take down all the religious statues, prayers and medals that adorn John Paul's crib. Afterwards Karen walks with me to the car and certifies that the car seat I purchased months ago is inserted correctly. Next step: homeward bound.

The most wonderful feeling in the world is walking through the front door with my son in my arms. It is a day I have longed for. I cannot believe it... My family is home, together under one roof.

Chapter Seven

Wisdom

Turn your wounds into wisdom

Oprah Winfrey

John Paul enjoying his birthday cake

John Paul's First Birthday
June 4, 1995

Decorations dangle from the ceiling, balloons float throughout the house. I watch cars begin to pull up the driveway. John Paul is on top form with toys strewed everywhere. He sits in the middle of the foyer with his new friend, Bonkers, a bright orange round creature with long lime green suction legs. When turned on Bonkers goes berserk, bouncing around on his six skinny legs.

The name fits, he drives me bonkers, but John Paul enjoys his craziness so I sacrifice my sanity.

Everyone who is part of and helped sustain John Paul's life is invited. He does not realize the significance of this day, but for me it is monumental. The doorbell rings, and the guests begin to arrive. John Paul stays in the middle of the foyer flashing a smile to those who enter. The decorated boxes and bags that gather on the couch spark his curiosity as does the house full of people.

I place John Paul in his highchair; his eyes scan all the people standing in front of him. He is unsure of what is happening; his bottom lip begins to quiver, that is until he sees the cake with a candle and hears the people begin to sing. *Happy birthday to you, happy birthday to you, happy birthday John Paul, happy birthday to you.* A smile widens across his face, he claps his hands and kicks his feet. I place the cake in front of him, kiss him on the top of his head and tell him to make a wish and blow out the candle. He takes a deep breath and blows with all his might. The flame vanishes, the group surrounding John Paul cheers, he smiles at his accomplishment. His index finger touches his lip, he is in deep thought. He eyes the cake; suddenly he digs his hands into the cake, scoops it up in the palms of his hands and shoves it into his mouth. Cake and icing plaster his face from his chin to the tip of his nose, even his long lashes flutter with white and blue frosting. I stand back and let him enjoy the moment as I absorb every detail of this happy occasion.

Later that evening, I walk into John Paul's room, sit in the rocker and watch him sleep. The moonlight cascades through the window casting a subtle glow on my son. I think back a year ago, the events of the past begin to replay in my mind. The past reminds me of the burden the future holds, this journey is far from over.

October 1994

I walk down the cold fluorescent corridor of the hospital. In my arms is John Paul, now four- months- old. I open the door to the first floor waiting room. Through the glass window, I see patients being prepped for surgery. My body is numb with fear. This could be it, the last time I hold my son. Each time the nurse calls a patient, I hold my breath. Finally, she approaches. Her arms reach out. Instinctively I tighten my grasp. She pulls John Paul out of my arms. He screams, his eyes plead, *Why are you letting her take me away? Save me!* I will never forget the look in John Paul's eyes when I let the nurse take him away from me. I hear his cry through the closed door. I cannot take it; I exit the room, walk into the hallway and cry.

The second stage of the Norwood Procedure concentrates on blood flow to the middle part of the body, of the three stages it is the least complicated. However, that does not in any way lessen the severity and complications associated with the procedure.

Annette, our families and I wait in the same waiting room we did for the previous surgery. The scene is familiar; we know what to expect and realize the wait will be long. I find myself going through the same routine I did just months ago: praying and pacing. Repetition does not make the wait easier, if anything I believe it is harder this time. Sister Dennis enters the waiting room and patiently waits with me and Annette. I look at the clock on the wall; my stomach begins to churn. John Paul has been in surgery longer than he was last time; worry overtakes me, my pacing increases as does my praying. Annette walks up to me, places her arms around my waist and lays her head on my chest. Her body trembles. I squeeze her tightly, lead her over to two chairs where we sit hand in hand and continue our wait.

"George family."

Reflexes jolt me out of my chair; my feet move quickly tugging the rest of my body to catch up. "Did you call the George family?"

The volunteer scans her paper. "Yes sir, Dr. Harmon will be in shortly."

Minutes seem like hours, but at last I see Dr. Harmon enter the surgical waiting room. The smile on his face triggers a sigh of relief. Annette and I listen intently, the news is great, the surgery was successful, no complications. John Paul is in recovery and will be in PICU soon.

Previously John Paul was in NICU and the adult ICU, this time he is in PICU, Pediatric Intensive Care Unit. The unit consists of one large room with beds stationed throughout. There are only two other children inside the dimly lit room. I remember what John Paul looked like after his first surgery, that vision intact, I prepare for the worse. At first, all I see are machines, just like before, providing life to my son. I hold my breath and walk closer. Relief expels at the sight of John Paul, but he looks remarkably well compared to before. His skin is rosy, and his face is swollen but not to the point of where he is unrecognizable. I stand and look at him; Annette is by my side. I am thrilled, yet guarded. I remember the complications after his first surgery and the out of control roller coaster Annette and I rode for almost two months. I block the thoughts and focus on the present.

Thankfully, the complications are minor and within two weeks, John Paul returns home. Every time a hurdle is cleared, I cannot help but think of the next one; it is knowledge forever etched in my mind. I know the next hurdle will undoubtedly be the hardest to clear. The third surgery is the final stage of the Norwood Procedure. This stage routes blood to the lower part of the body and determines if half a heart can withstand the pressure. This knowledge plays on my mind constantly, but I try to take advantage of every minute I have with my son. Everyday is precious, a gift.

At one month old John Paul became addicted to the vivid vision produced by the television. In NICU the nurses, unable to pacify him, placed a television in front of his crib and played Disney videos and sing-a-longs. Everything from Mary Poppins to the Jungle Book occupied his attention; however his favorite was Song of the South's Zip-A-Dee-Doo-Dah. During his stay in the hospital after his second surgery, once again the television was the tool used to pacify him. At home he still loves to be placed in front of the television. I find myself buying every Disney video I can find and cannot wait until he is well enough to take him to Disney World.

November 1994 until July 1995 is indescribable. Thanksgiving and the first Christmas with my son is like no other that I have ever experienced. The joy of Christmas is truly the best when experienced through the eyes of a child. The family celebrates the birth of Jesus with sincere thanksgiving for sparing John Paul's life. Every holiday seems to hold more meaning now that John Paul is with me, and it goes without saying what a milestone his first birthday was. However on August 15, 1995 the smooth sailing comes to a turbulent stop. On this evening John Paul goes to bed around seven and sleeps well until he wakes up at five in the morning crying uncontrollably. Annette and I both try to calm him but nothing works. Annette phones the pediatrician who advises her to give John Paul Tylenol and a warm bath. After the warm bath John Paul vomits. I admit, Annette and I are not grounded when John Paul becomes ill, too many what ifs stir through our minds. Annette calls the pediatrician again. This time his advice is to take John Paul to the hospital.

John Paul screams in agony the entire trip. The emergency room is packed; I cannot have John Paul wait, plus he does not need to be around sickness. I rush to the nurse's desk and explain the situation. Luckily the nurse is understanding and places us in a room. I lay John Paul on the table, he squirms and cries with pain. I try cradling his legs to his stomach, but this does not help. A nurse enters the room takes his vitals and listens as Annette details what has transpired. I can no longer take seeing my son in pain, I ask the nurse to please get a doctor.

Two days lapse; observation is continuous but a cause for the pain has not been determined. John Paul is being feed intravenously; however he spits up small amounts of yellowish green fluid and begins to have the dry heaves. An x-ray of his abdomen shows a small bowel obstruction. Emergency surgery is scheduled. Dr. Shaw, the surgeon who operated on his bowel previously, will conduct the surgery. I do not want my son to go to surgery, the risks are too high. I call my doctor friend John to get his advice. Unfortunately his wife Linda states John is on his way to a medical conference. I explain John Paul's circumstance. Linda tells me to hold tight, John's plane is suppose to land within minutes, she will try to have him paged at the airport and have him call the room. This is in the dark ages, a time when a cell phone was not in everyone's hand. A doctor enters and asks for a signature for consent. I ask for a little more time. I know it is a long shot, but I pray John will call. Within a half hour the phone rings; amazingly John heard the page in O'Hara Airport.

"You have no other choice. The source of the pain has to be determined."

Annette signs the anesthesia consent form, and I sign the operation consent. John Paul is rushed to surgery.

Scar tissue from the stomach surgery in 1994 is determined to be the cause of John Paul's pain and vomiting. Thankfully, it is not anything more serious, and on August 22, 1995 John Paul is discharged.

The episode brought about the realization that John Paul must be in good health and great shape before he has his third stage. The cold weather of North Carolina is a hindrance to John Paul's health. Fall and winter bring cold and flu season. Unfortunately, for this reason John Paul remains dormant indoors during this time of year. I want to be proactive, get him to a warmer climate, a place where he can play outside, enjoy the sunlight and grow. Annette and I contemplate what to do.

Growing up I longed for independence to make my own decisions. Now, I wish someone could make this hard choice for me. Oprah Winfrey once said, "Turn your wounds into wisdom." I realize my past experiences can only make me wiser in dealing with the obstacles of the future. In my heart, I know what I need to do for my son, move to a warmer climate, but I dread the thought of leaving family and friends. I know the move will be excruciating for Annette. She and her family are very close and have never been separated. In addition, I have an established business that I have nurtured for years.

From Annette:

One of the hardest decisions I ever faced was whether to pack up and move to Florida. I am a mountain girl to the bone and the thought of leaving my home state disturbs me. I will not miss the superficial things, change of seasons or rural beauty; it is much deeper than that. I am petrified to leave my family. My parents exhibit unconditional love; they have cared for my sister and brother for over twenty years until their medical needs necessitated nursing care. They have already lost my brother to the rare disease, Friedrich's Ataxia, and now they continuously remain by my sister's bedside in the nursing home. During John Paul's illness many have asked how I endure the stress and obstacles associated with a sick child. My response is always the same, God, faith, and the best role models, my parents. I have watched my parents give total devotion to my brother and sister, doing whatever it takes to make sure they receive the best possible care. That is what Derek and I want for John Paul. We have to do what is best for our son in preparation for his third surgery, which is why we have decided to leave everything and move to Florida.

It is mid-October, the U-Haul is packed. Darkness has not given way to light as the caravan of cars pull out of the driveway. Derek's family decides to make the move to Florida, which offers some comfort, but it will not completely fill the void of my family. My spirit is broken; I choke back tears as I drive the shadowy road. Daylight creeps up; I reclaim my perspective with the image of John Paul in the rearview mirror.

From Derek:

The move has been tough but I will endure anything for my son. Everything is new and different; however, the landscape reminds me of my homeland, South Africa. The warm weather is a great benefit, almost everyday John Paul is able to be outside and play. The two of us are inseparable. He is constantly on my heels following me around the house and everywhere I go. One thing I have noticed since moving to Florida is that John Paul has a natural talent for swinging the golf club. It is amazing how God works, He provides my son with a gift that he will be able to use. Golf is not strenuous; it is a sport he will be able to enjoy. I try to nurture his talent and take him to the driving range and golf course on a regular basis. I notice a stubborn streak that breeds his strong willpower and strength within. I sometimes wonder if I only had a quarter of his willpower and strength how different I would be.

The question of when the next surgery will be constantly surfaces to the forefront of my mind. Just before John Paul's third birthday, I receive the answer. The cardiologist feels it is time. He is pleased with his progress and his growth; however, I am not sure I am ready for what lies ahead. Knowing the time is here makes my nights sleepless. The million-dollar question that now plagues me is where to have the surgery. The complications from the first stage surgery haunt me. I do not know if the hospital in North Carolina is equipped to handle the serious third and final stage. Dr. Norwood, the doctor who invented the procedure, pioneered the surgery at Philadelphia Children's. The reputation of the hospital is outstanding. Annette and I seriously debate the pro and cons of taking John Paul to Philadelphia. The primary reservation, the doctors at Philadelphia have never seen or administered to John Paul, whereas Dr. Harmon's knowledge of my son and his condition is indisputable. After much contemplation, we decide to take John Paul back to North Carolina.

Chapter Eight

Faith

Faith is taking the first step even when you don't see the whole staircase.

Martin Luther King Jr.

John Paul and Tyler Perry

From Annette:
Madea AKA Tyler Perry

John Paul loves Tyler Perry movies, especially Madea. He constantly spurts out Madea's one-liners, so much that Derek and I actually think we live with Madea.

Whenever I sense John Paul has a passion for someone I strive my best to connect the two. Hence our journey to Jacksonville, Florida to see *Madea's Big Happy Family*. Mr. Perry's agent explains that she will provide tickets and a possible quick meet and greet with Mr. Perry, and we are thrilled with the opportunity. The venue for the play is bustling. We pick up our tickets and the usher shows us to our seats. My dad has come along with me and John Paul since Derek is away on business. Our eyes pop wide open when the usher stops just a few rows back from the stage.

"Are you kidding me?" John Paul asks, his eyes sparkling with delight.

I check the seat and row numbers and happily confirm the location. We sit down only briefly before my cell phone rings. The gentleman on the other end explains that he is Mr. Perry's assistant and ask that we meet him at the right side of the stage. At this point John Paul is estatic. We arrive at the stage and in just a few seconds a man, who introduces himself as Ron, takes us behind the curtain. We pause momentarily, and John Paul listens intently as the man explains what is about to take place.

"Mr. Perry will be arriving shortly. Once he arrives he will meet with you for a few minutes in his dressing room. Before he gets in costume he has prayer with the cast members. He would like for you guys to join him for the prayer as well. Is that okay?"

"We would be honored," I say as I look at John Paul and smile.

We walk back toward his dressing room and wait. I hand my dad the camera and ask him to take a picture or two of John Paul and Mr. Perry. In the distance I see Mr. Perry coming down the wide corridor. John Paul's eyes catch sight of him, his smiles widens as he approaches. Introductions are made and Mr. Perry invites us into his dressing room.

Once inside the first thing John Paul notices is the Madea costume. The sight of that puts him in Madea mode. Mr. Perry offers a chair, and John Paul sits down while Mr. Perry kneels beside him. The two begin chatting.

"Did he insult you Cora? Did he insult the WWJD?" John Paul spurts out in his high-pitched Madea voice.

As John Paul continues his Madea impressions, Mr. Perry is unable to contain his laughter. John Paul then informs Mr. Perry that he wants to be in his next movie and with assurance Mr. Perry tells him he will get him a line.

"One line? Man I need five or six lines!" He shoots back still in Madea mode.

He laughs and tells him he will see what he can do.

Mr. Perry has been briefed on John Paul's situation but I hand him a YouTube video of John Paul which explains some of the obstacles he has been through.

The conversation flows effortlessly and after a few minutes Mr. Perry ask us to join him and his cast in prayer. We follow him out to the corridor where the cast of his play is waiting. He introduces John Paul and the warm reception is marvelous. We enter the circle and join hands. Mr. Perry begins to pray and the amazing thing: he prays eloquently for my son. Tears stream down my face. I open my eyes briefly to see John Paul's hand clasped tightly in the man's he has admired from afar.

Following the prayer John Paul says good-bye to Mr. Perry, and we are ushered back to our seats. John Paul can hardly sit still. He is chattering continuously about his conversation with Mr. Perry until the curtain parts.

We absolutely loved the play. Madea definitely has a mouth with a meaning. The pistol-packing grandma has a way of letting us know that we are not alone in our trials and challenges and always brings us back to our faith.

During one scene, Madea calls out John Paul's name. John Paul looks at me in disbelief. "John Paul I think you'll remember this song." Madea begins singing Bye Bye Miss American Pie. John Paul stands and waves and the crowd cheers. In his a special way Tyler Perry, aka Madea, includes John Paul in the show. However his inclusion does not stop there. The final curtain call Mr. Perry arrives out on the stage, out of his Madea drag, and begins introducing his cast. In a moment that will forever be etched in John Paul's memory Mr. Perry asks John Paul to stand. Mr. Perry tells the audience about my son. He encompasses all John Paul had been through, the audience cheers at his words, and John Paul stands taller than ever. Talk about someone remembering his roots and the true meaning of faith, love and compassion... Never in my life have I met someone as real as Tyler Perry.

Within the next couple of days Mr. Perry's office called and took down all John Paul's contact information. "You are now part of our family," the nice lady told me. John Paul was thrilled with that statement. "Mom that means we'll be invited to Madea's next family reunion!"

June 1997

The fire-engine red suburban is packed; John Paul sits securely in his car seat. It's early morning; where we are going has not been discussed; all he knows is we are going on a trip. For some reason he thinks we are going to Disney. This tears at my heart, how I wish that was the final destination, but it is not. The drive will take a good eleven hours to Annette's parents in North Carolina where we will stay the night. Every few minutes I glance into the rearview mirror. John Paul who is still in his mint green pajamas watches a video, his dark hair is longer than most three year olds', but he likes it and so do I. It reminds me of Samson whose miraculous strength came from his long hair. When our eyes meet, he flashes an innocent smile, which drives the dagger deeper into my heart. There are so many emotions bottled up inside me, anxiety, hurt, helplessness. I begin to wonder if this will be the last week I will be able to see him, touch him. No parent should have to experience this. The demon of distress slowly eats away at my being no matter how hard I try to avert it. The only redeeming feature is my faith, without it, I would be six feet under.

When we turn into his grandparents' driveway John Paul claps his hands and shouts. "Grandma! Papaw!" He is so happy to see his grandparents I can't help, but watch him. He poses for pictures and smiles, I smile back, but the thought of what tomorrow holds kills the joy of the moment.

As the morning arrives, Annette and I both find it hard to get out of bed. I walk into the family room, John Paul, an early-riser, is all ready and sitting on the floor watching Barney. I wish I could freeze time and not have to venture into this new day.

After breakfast we load into the SUV; John Paul wants to know where we are going and why his grandparents are not coming. I avoid his questions and change the subject. The drive is short, only about thirty minutes, but it is enough time for us to recite the rosary. John Paul's voice joins in unison with mine and Annette's as he annunciates each word. His voice reminds me of that of an angel.

I pull into the parking lot and find a space. I push John Paul's stroller, Annette's hand is tightly clasped around my arm. Reluctantly we enter the main admitting area, both of us cut up on the inside, yet our outward appearance remains strong for our son. Suddenly I hear my name being called from across the room. I look, and in the distance I see Sister Dennis. *What a blessing*, I think to myself. Since the day John Paul was born, she has been by his side in the hospital, visiting, praying, and encouraging us to rely on our faith and God. It is amazing how God works; he puts those we need in the right place at the right time. Her presence relieves some of the apprehension as we sit and wait.

"John Paul George," the nurse calls from the admitting desk.

We follow the nurse to the pediatric floor and enter a room. John Paul looks around and takes everything in, the bed with railings, the teal recliner, and the rolling wooden tray. By this point he is confused and afraid, I see it in his eyes.

"Look up here." I stand below the television mounted on the wall. "You have your very own television."

His demeanor lightens when his glance fixes on the television.

"Plus there's a VCR, so you can watch videos." I reach down, pick him up, place him in the middle of the bed and turn on the television.

Around one in the afternoon, a nurse enters the room, at the sight of her John Paul climbs off the bed and jumps onto my lap. She explains that she needs to get an IV started for the catheterization. She asks John Paul to hold out his arm, he tenses up; he remembers the procedure and starts to squirm. The nurse is not able to locate a vein, but she proceeds to prick his small arm. John Paul begins to cry. He shifts closer into my chest, in an attempt to get away from the needle. I have no choice, but to hold him down. John Paul realizes I am helping the nurse; he begins to slap me while screaming for me to make her stop.

I encompass him tightly, finally a vein pops up and with one last prick the nurse gets the IV going. His tears subside, but I see the frightfulness; he is so scared. My nerves are shot. I place John Paul on his bed; Annette sits down beside him and turns the television to one of his favorite shows.

Trying not to display my emotions, I leave the room and enter the men's room around the corner where I weep like a baby. I realize John Paul has lost faith in me. I am no longer his protector, his trust in me has slipped, the bond broken.

Doctors and nurses filter in and out the room the rest of the day. Around six in the evening his surgeon, Dr. Harmon, enters. He is very pleased with John Paul's progress. Most doctors keep a clear-cut doctor/patient relationship, but I can tell our son holds a special place in his heart. He gives Annette and I a sheet of paper to read, Request for Operation and/or Other Procedures. We have signed these forms in the past; a signature must be present before the procedure can take place. By signing this, I give the hospital permission to proceed with the catheterization. I read the risks and consequences, bleeding, infection, stroke, death. Right under there is a place for the alternatives to this procedure, the word "none" is scribbled on the line. Such drastic risks, but no alternative. With a lump the size of a baseball lodged in my throat I sign the form. Annette signs on the line beside my name as a witness and dates the form, June 23, 1997.

The next morning at eight forty, a man in pale green scrubs arrives to take John Paul down to the first floor for his catheterization. He stands behind a wheelchair, his hands positioned ready to push.

"If it's okay, I'll carry my son."

He gives a nod. I scoop up John Paul, who is already drowsy from the sedative given earlier, into my arms. Annette and I walk him down to the first floor. At the door, the man waits for us to kiss our son; with much apprehension I hand him over. We watch through the small glass window in the door until our son disappears from our sight. Neither of us says much on our walk back up to John Paul's room where we will wait.

I pace the floor, talk to family, watch television, anything to keep my mind occupied. The doctors assured Annette and me that everything would be fine during the procedure; however, when I think about the release form I know there is always that chance… Finally, after several hours the nurse informs us that John Paul is fine and will be coming to the room within the half hour.

Groggy, the nurses transfer him from the gurney to his bed. We lower our voices and let him rest, but he does not sleep long. He wakes up with a smile on his face and an appetite.

Tomorrow is the turning point for our family, the last stage of John Paul's three stages Norwood Procedure. Although the first stage is very important, most doctors say the third is the most crucial surgery, seeing if half of a heart can withstand the pressure of doing the work of a whole heart. Now the blood flow will be routed to the lower part of the body, linking all three stages together.

Dr. Harmon stops by after supper and discusses the findings of the catheterization; he is very pleased and states that John Paul is a good candidate for the final stage. While he explains what tomorrow will entail, John Paul sits in the middle of his bed and watches television, indifferent to what is being discussed. Once again, a release form is placed in front of me, this time for the open-heart surgery. I scan through the risks, bleeding, infection, risks of anesthesia, transfusion, stroke heart attack, death, kidney failure. Signing the paper I cannot fathom how many consequences associated with the surgery will actually happen to John Paul, but within twelve hours of the surgery, I soon find out.

Chapter Nine

Fortitude

As a camel beareth labor, and heat, and hunger, and thirst through deserts of sand and fainteth not; so the fortitude of a man shall sustain him through all perils.

John Ruskin

John Paul helping the Benjamin School football team

August 2009

Adam Sandler as Bobby Boucher in The Waterboy is hilarious, a movie John Paul thoroughly enjoys. Thanks to a good friend, John Paul is now the waterboy, or as he prefers to be called the H20 boy, for the Benjamin School Varsity football team. These young men tower over John Paul but with hearts the size of a football field, they make him feel ten feet tall.

I do not know what to expect from John Paul, I mean all he has to do is run the water out to his teammates and head back to the sidelines. Before the game we go into the team locker room, greet the players and their great coach, Ron Ream. We head out to the sidelines and I take a seat on the bench with John Paul stationed behind me fiddling with the water bottles. In the background I hear someone shouting John Paul's name. I turn to see John Paul enthusiastically smiling and waving. I follow his gaze and marvel to see Jack Nicklaus standing and waving at John Paul. Mr. Nicklaus, whose grandson plays for the team, has also infused kindness into John Paul's life which is evident from his wonderful quote.

John Paul finishes his duty and takes a seat next to me awaiting the arrival of the team. The upbeat music begins, John Paul rushes to the sideline and high fives the players as they run onto the field. I watch the two team captains motion for John Paul to accompany them to middle of the field for the coin toss. The announcer introduces the captains and John Paul as part of the team. The crowd cheers at his introduction, and John Paul gives a wave to acknowledge his new fan club. One of the captains whisper their selection into John Paul's ear and I watch him mouth the call. The crowd cheers, the captains pat John Paul on the back as they select to receive.

The first time out is called, and I watch John Paul grab two water bottles and tag along with the other water boy to the middle of the field. I expect to see him hand the bottle to one of the players for a quick drink, but John Paul's unique personality takes over. Within a blink of an eye, John Paul takes the water bottle and begins to squirt one of the big defensive players on the back of his neck and head. With the second water bottle he spatters water on the front of another player's jersey. Finally, after he has cooled the players off he allows them to each take a drink before scurrying for the sidelines. The remainder of the season proceeded like the first game. The crowd started to look forward to timeouts, wondering what antics John Paul had up his sleeve to cool the players off.

However, John Paul while upholding his duties as H2O boy still found time to give Coach Ream advice while on the sidelines which we found out about at the athletic banquet. Coach Ream set the scene.

"During one of the games I was standing on the sidelines contemplating what to do when I felt a tug on my sleeve. I looked down to find John Paul standing beside me, his eyes smiling with anticipation."

"Coach, I got a play for you! You've only got one option. Throw a Hail Mary!"

Coach Ream stood behind the podium and smiled. "I told him good call. For that outstanding advice and the motivation instilled in our team, I present the revered Coaches Award to John Paul George."

6-25-97 Nursing Notes
8:00 am To OR via dad's arms
accompanied by transporter.

Reluctantly I release John Paul to the surgical nurse, the transfer is excruciating. This albatross has haunted me for the past three years, day and night; it has constantly been in the back of my mind. It hits me at different times, watching John Paul hit golf balls, teaching him to swim, or as I watch him sleep. It is terrible; I can be having a great day with my son, suddenly what lays ahead pops into my head, and it is hard to shake the reality of the future. Today the future that I have dreaded is here, the final stage of the Norwood Procedure, and it scares the life out of me.

The surgical waiting room, a place too painfully familiar, is the same place I waited during John Paul's first and second stage Norwood surgeries. Annette and I walk in and find our families sitting in the back right corner of the large room. Everywhere I look, I see people waiting, waiting for news. Everyone in the room is dealing with their own worry. In a way, I feel as though

I am not alone, but that does not provide comfort. Although the room is full, there is little noise, only the muffled sounds of people whispering. Some people flip through magazines, some watch the silent television, others talk to those around them and others sit with their eyes closed most likely talking to the man upstairs.

Annette and I know the routine; we sit hand in hand and begin waiting, a journey that will take the entire day. I wish I were ignorant about the particulars of the surgery; sometimes ignorance is bliss. However, I do know and understand my son's chest will be exposed; a heart lung machine will sustain his life for most of the day. This realization shakes my spirit. I think back three years ago, the angel sent to me in my time of distress. I watch the corridor, look around the waiting room in hopes of his return; I could use a little reassurance.

The glow of Annette's face drains as the day wears on. I try to remain upbeat. I give her hand a tight squeeze and tell her everything is going to be fine. I remind her of the network of prayers going up for our son. Since his birth, people of all denominations, small country churches, big cathedrals, have united in prayer for John Paul. The prayers do not stop at the boundaries of our town; they spread wide and far across the states and around the world. The power of prayer is phenomenal; one look at John Paul and I see the authenticity of the statement.

The hours drag. I find myself on edge, continuously watching the hands of the clock move slower than normal. I flip through magazines and books, but nothing helps alleviate the tension building inside of me. I occasionally walk to the volunteer who updates families to see if there is any news. Her response is the same each time, "Still in surgery."

By the eighth hour the waiting game is getting to me, I am in dire straits. I cannot sit still, eat or drink. I pace constantly around the room trying to keep my mind occupied.

Three hours later, I see him at the entrance of the door in his green surgical attire.

"There's Dr. Harmon." At the sound of my words, I leap out of my chair.

My knees are wobbly, my eyes search the doctors' face for an indication of how things went, and all I see is strain. He stops in front of me and Annette, our family encircles behind us.

"The surgery went well."

The words are music to my ears. Instant relief erupts from my eyes, I feel the tears stream down my face. Annette throws herself into me, three years of emotions explode, and we stand tightly enfolded. It is difficult to describe how I feel, the only word that comes to mind is relief, relief that the third and final surgery is behind us. Finally, the albatross that has plagued my family's being for three years is over. Gradually we release ourselves, turn to the doctor and listen to the limited details of the surgery.

Dr. Harmon explains that John Paul has been through turmoil, his system is in shock, and it will take time for his vitals to recover. He is still in the operating room, once stable John Paul will be moved to PICU (Pediatric Intensive Care Unit) where we will be able to visit in an hour. Although we already know it, he reminds us that recovery is crucial, the next twenty to forty-eight hours are critical. I am relieved the surgery is over; surgery is the primary hurdle, big misconception. Surgery is major, but aftercare determines the outcome of a successful surgery. Unfortunately, this is a lesson I learned the hard way.

Annette and I transfer from the surgical waiting room to the PICU waiting area. The room is much smaller, only about twenty chairs, with a pay phone and glass window allowing a view into the hallway. A nurse arrives at the door, Annette and I follow her into PICU.

John Paul's bed is in the middle of the room, directly in front of the nurse's station. I stand back. Is the same little boy I carried to the operating room this morning? His features are different. His swollen face looks like it will pop at any moment, his eyes are puffy and crusted shut, and he is bruised black and blue. Annette carefully inches closer, kisses him on his forehead and tells him she loves him. I am still frozen in my tracks. This is the worse I have ever seen him look, I can't get pass it. I am responsible. I signed the release form.

Annette tugs at me. "Come talk to him, he needs to hear your voice. It will comfort him."

I shake the doubt from my mind and focus on John Paul's healing. For the next fifteen minutes, I sit beside his bed and talk about the things we love to do together. I describe the golf we will play at the club back in Florida, movies we will see like George of the Jungle. I tell him I cannot wait to take him to the Aero Club, a landing strip near our home, and watch the planes take off and land. The nurse informs me that the visitation time is up. I hate to leave him. Annette and I both give him a kiss and leave the room. We go back down to the PICU waiting room where we will stay until we are able to visit again.

It is eleven o'clock, only Annette and I remain in the waiting room. The chairs have cushioned seats, but the arms are wooden and hard. I try endlessly to get comfortable so I can get a little sleep. Finally, I doze off. My sleep is restless; events of the day play out in my dream. I hear my name being called, thinking it is a dream I ignore it; however I hear my name again this time it is louder. Slowly I open my eyes and try to figure out where I am; in a haze I see Dr. Harmon.

"John Paul is going back to the OR. He is losing large amounts of blood from the chest tube."

Thrust into a nightmare, I can hardly think straight. "Are there any other options?"

He shakes his head, "No, it is imperative the bleeding be stopped."

Although I know the doctor's response will be noncommittal, I ask, "Is he going to be okay?" All I want is reassurance, someone to say yes your son is going to be fine.

"There's risk with every surgery, this is no different. The risks are greater because of the traumatic surgery John Paul had only hours ago."

I look at Annette, she cannot believe this either, her head rest in her hands. Without looking up, she asks, "Can we see him?"

"He will be going shortly, but you may stay with him until we are ready."

Again, we wait this time at John Paul's bedside until he leaves PICU. I can hardly bear to watch him leave again to go to surgery. I start to argue silently with myself. *What in the world was I thinking? I should have gone with my initial instinct and taken him to Philadelphia or Boston. I was wrong for not going to a larger children's hospital. Aftercare is so important. Did I not learn anything from previous experiences? Is this hospital going to be able to handle my son's condition?*

Annette and I go back to the waiting room. Exhaustion settles in, neither of us can keep our eyes open, we nod off only to wake every few minutes. At two in the morning, Dr. Harmon stops by and informs us John Paul is on his way back to PICU. The surgery was successful. The bleeding has stopped. The news is great, but to be honest, I am afraid to show any signs of relief for fear of what is around the next corner.

Two thirty in the morning I send Annette back to waiting room to get some rest. The nurse encourages me to do the same, visiting hours ended long ago. I advise the nurse from this point forward neither Annette nor I will be adhering to the visitation schedule. One of us will be with John Paul at all times. I am sure she does not like my self-made rules, but with my son's well-being at stake this is not the time to worry about what others think. I pull up one of the rolling stools and sit directly next to John Paul's bed. I watch in silence everything done to John Paul. The nurse begins her vitals check; she takes John Paul's temperature, blood pressure, and checks for a pulse in each extremity.

She stops and pauses, her hand moves up and down John Paul's left leg.

"Is something wrong?" I ask.

"I can't find a pulse in the left leg." She takes her stethoscope and listens for a pulse. She remarks that the leg is very cold, tense, and discolored.

"Why would that happen?" I get up and clasp my hand around the calf muscle, which is cold; I move my hand to his thigh, same thing.

"It may be the arterial line (A-line). That is a very small tube that is placed in a blood vessel. We use it to check blood pressure, draw blood samples and check oxygen saturations."

"Can it be removed?"

"It can, but it will need to be placed elsewhere."

My thoughts chase each other. *How did this happen? What if the pulse doesn't return? No circulation means the leg will die. Dear God, my son may lose his leg.* Disbelief shudders through me. Scenarios of my son not being able to walk, run or play his favorite sport, golf, begins to unnerve me. I cannot help thinking this is something that could have been avoided.

I intently watch the doctor change the arterial line, after he finishes I ask the nurse for a blanket. Methodically I wrap the left leg with the blanket and begin to massage trying to revive circulation. I massage his leg so much that my hands become numb. Although the leg begins to warm there is still no pulse. The "what ifs" rage through my mind and drive me crazy, so I focus all my energy on rubbing and massaging my son's lifeless leg.

The only way I tell time is by shift change, a new nurse arrives around six thirty. The two nurses discuss the events since surgery and the entries on John Paul's chart. I listen and relive the events of the nightmarish night; I hope the light of day brings a better day for John Paul.

Lab results arrive just before the nurses finish their charting. Concern trickles across the face of each nurse.

"How are the results?"

The two look at each other. The nurse comes over and shows me the results.

"John Paul's liver enzymes are extremely elevated."

"What does that mean?"

"It can be many things, I will notify the doctor and he will be in shortly."

6-26-97 Nursing/Doctor Notes:

8:45 a.m. Significant bleeding overnight requiring re-exploration of chest. Chest tube drainage less, slowed considerably. Left leg forced art line removal because of obstruction of femoral artery. Left leg now worse, without pulse, and tense. Suspect thrombus (blood clot) in femoral artery. Liver enzymes grossly elevated, PT (blood clotting time) greatly elevated. The renal function has slowly been deteriorating with a urine output of 1 cc/ hr. Cardiac function is good. Responds to verbal stimuli. I suspect that coagulopathy (defection in body's ability to clot blood) reflects hepatic (liver) function. Kidney function will be important.

I take a break from massaging John Paul's leg and sit on the rolling stool, depleted. I hear the automatic doors open, I look up and see Annette. I know she is coming, hoping John Paul is improving; I force a slight smile as she nears.

She leans in, gives me a gentle kiss on the cheek, walks over, and kisses John Paul on his forehead.

"How is he?"

It is bad enough to have to tell her about John Paul's leg, but now on top of that there is the issue with the liver enzymes.

"Why's his leg wrapped up?"

I see the apprehension begin to tighten her muscles. She reaches under the blanket and touches his leg then touches his right leg.

"Derek, his left leg is a lot cooler than his right. What's wrong?"

I place my arm around her shoulder and pull her away from John Paul's bed.

"Early this morning the nurse noticed John Paul's left leg was cold, and she couldn't find a pulse. Evidently the line used to get blood samples, check blood pressure and oxygen levels injured his leg."

Annette's face is ashen. "What does that mean? Is he going to lose his leg?"

Tears begin to flow effortlessly.

I enclose my arms around her tightly. "I am not sure; I hope the blanket will keep it warm, I've been massaging trying to revive circulation. It is a bit warmer, we will have to wait and see if a pulse returns." I hesitate, I do not want to tell her about the blood work, but I cannot keep anything from her. "There's more."

"I've only been asleep a few hours. How can there be more?"

I release my embrace, step back until we are facing each other. "John Paul's liver enzymes are too high."

Her brow crinkles trying to understand. "Can't they give him some medicine for that?"

"I am not sure. First they have to find out why the levels are elevated, the doctor should be here any minute."

Annette looks over at his fragile still body, machines breathing for him.

"How can John Paul endure all this?"

I shake my head at her words; I too am at a lost.

Confusion is a look I definitely do not want to see on a doctor's face, especially in a time of crisis. My nervous tension unravels at Dr. Harmon's demeanor and words.

"To be honest, I am not sure why the liver enzymes are elevated, it can be one of many things. I have ordered an ultrasound of the heart to see if there is a connection. I will know more once the scan is complete."

"When will the ultrasound be done?" I ask.

"X-ray will be up within the next thirty minutes." The doctor examines John Paul, listens to his heart, pinches his fingernails and toenails measuring the blood flow to the limbs. When he gets to the left leg there is nothing, the only warmth is from the blanket, the blood flow is void. Dr. Harmon sees the fretfulness that engulfs Annette and me; he places his arms around us both.

"Hang in there," he pauses. "And pray."

I nod, unable to speak, the lump in my throat will not allow me, but my thoughts still race. Concern inflicts every part of me. I am petrified that the liver is not functioning because the heart is not pumping enough blood to the lower part of the body.

The x-ray doctor enters PICU, Dr. Harmon gives him instructions then walks over to the nurse's station. The doctor rolls the heavy machine next to John Paul. Annette cannot handle the pressure and decides to go to the waiting room; I stay. The machine takes a few minutes to warm up; finally, the doctor pushes record and starts the scan. I watch the monitor and his face. My mind reverts to Annette's first sonogram and the technician's face when she found the defect. I am on pins and needles, my heart racing; I sit silently until I am no longer able to take it.

"How does the heart look?"

He does not answer right away, he continues with the scan. I am on the brink, I want to shout, "Hey that's my son, have a little compassion!" I realize I am overreacting and settle down and allow him time to look. I wait a few minutes.

I clear my throat. "How does the heart look?"

He looks a bit longer, and then responds, "The heart looks fine, I do not see any abnormalities, but Dr. Harmon will review the tape."

There is a certain sense of relief knowing the heart is okay, but I see the puzzlement on the faces of the nurses and residents who watch. The doctor begins to shut down the machine. He cannot leave; the underlying reason for the elevated liver enzymes has not been resolved. My emotions swell.

"Can you please scan the liver?"

The doctor, evidently not used to taking directives from a family member, ignores me. I reassert my request, "Please, before you leave, scan the liver."

He proceeds to inform me the doctor only ordered a scan of the heart. He will need orders from Dr. Harmon in order to scan the liver. I look over my shoulder; Dr. Harmon is no longer at the nurse's station. I cannot wait for him to be paged so I plead to him, "Please, I beg you; I will take full responsibility, just take a look at the liver."

He hears my direness and agrees to scan the liver. He squirts gel onto John Paul's abdomen and locates the liver with the scanner. Carefully he watches the monitor; his eyes remain fixed on the screen, his hand moves locating every angle. Without a word, he places the scanner back into the slot.

"I'll be right back."

My eyes follow him over to the nurse's station. I watch him pick up the phone, speak into it, then walk back in my direction.

"Dr. Harmon will be right in."

Within minutes, Dr. Harmon is at John Paul's bed. The two converse while they view the findings. I feel the tension. Dr. Harmon turns to me, "John Paul has a clot in his liver; this is the reason for the elevated enzymes."

I think, *A blood clot? That can be dissolved with a blood thinner...* "Can't the clot be dissolved with a blood thinner?"

"I'm afraid it is not that easy. It is serious; if John Paul is given a blood thinner, he could bleed to death due to his recent surgery. With the rapid deterioration of his liver functions, John Paul is at risk of going into shock, plus his kidneys may not be able to withstand the pressure."

I let out a deep sigh, close my eyes and think, *Dear God, what are we going to do? It kills me to look at John Paul. Just days ago he was hitting golf balls, enjoying life to the fullest, and now...*

I can't passively sit back and just let things happen. I begin to roam the floors of the ICU like a madman, assertively encouraging each doctor to find out what can be done to save my son. Things move too slowly; slow motion does not work for me, not when my son's life is at stake. I do not remember the last time I had something to eat, yet my energy level is high; I am running on pure adrenaline. I go back and forth to the offices of the doctors and residents. I hammer them continuously and persuade them to call Boston, Philadelphia, Miami, and all major medical facilities to find out how to treat the clot in John Paul's liver. I enter the PICU doctor's office and together we search the internet for answers; surely, one of these avenues will yield a positive response. Unfortunately, a blood thinner, is the only known solution. This occurrence is such a rarity, the hospitals cannot believe the stroke of bad luck, no one is able to help.

My adrenaline rush subsides, Annette and I sit by John Paul's bedside and wait. No words are spoken, in deep thought we stare at our son. I am sure the same worrisome ideas that float through my mind are the same for Annette. The confines of a hospital allow for a great deal of time to ponder and think. I can't help but think back to the past year and a half during which time I have tried to help John Paul become stronger. I learned a great deal about the body while serving in the South African Military where I was a PTI (physical training instructor). The knowledge has been beneficial in helping my son. On a child's level I encouraged John Paul to do exercises and brief aerobic fitness hoping to get his body in shape for the surgery. I never told my family or friends the motivation for the daily exercise routine, but I knew it was crucial for John Paul's stamina and strength.

Minutes seem like hours, I converse continuously with the doctors in hopes they may find a new remedy. My concern now is not only the liver, but also how much time is left until the kidneys begin to fail. Time is short, the nurse notifies me that the urine output has diminished drastically; this is worrisome.

Pediatric Renal Dialysis is quickly notified, as are Annette and I, as to what is about to happen. My son is going to be put on dialysis. I can't help but think about the people I have known who have been on dialysis; the outcome has not been positive. To me this seems like the beginning of the end. So many machines are providing him life, will he ever be able to survive without their assistance.

Chapter Ten

Willpower

We can be tired, weary and emotionally distraught, but after spending time alone with God, we find that He injects into our bodies energy, power and strength.

Charles Stanley

John Paul and Tiger

March 2009

Willpower is definitely a word that applies to John Paul. Once he sets his mind to something he doesn't retreat until he succeeds.

As long as I can remember, he has always dreamed of meeting Tiger Woods.

Loving the game and actually being very good at it, he visualizes a Skins Game between he and Tiger. He constantly tugs at his mom's ear about his desire to meet Tiger. I often hear her pacify him by saying *maybe someday*, but in our private conversations we discuss the remote possibility that will happen. In private Annette is trying, without much luck, every avenue to make John Paul's dream come true.

Thursday morning after mass we are talking to a good friend about the Arnold Palmer Invitational which is being played in Orlando. Back in the car I nonchalantly mention to Annette that Tiger is playing the tournament and maybe a tournament official could help John Paul meet Tiger. Once we arrive home, Annette takes the telephone, goes into the room and closes the door. In a few minutes she calls me into the room.

"I left a message for the tournament director at the Arnold Palmer and briefly told him about John Paul and his desire to meet Tiger. Don't know if he will call back, but we will see. You never know."

Within twenty minutes of leaving the message the phone rings and Annette dashes back into room and closes the door. About twenty minutes later she calls me into the room.

"I spoke to the tournament director's assistant, Tiffany. Oh my gosh! She is so sweet. She wants us to plan to come to the tournament tomorrow morning early and she will meet us there. She said she can't promise but she is going to try her best to get John Paul to meet Tiger."

We walk back into the kitchen where John Paul is eating breakfast. Annette shares the news with John Paul who jumps out of his chair and does a Tiger fist punch.

Before the sun rises we are out at the putting green watching the professionals putt under the bright florescent lights. Tiffany comes and introduces herself and takes us inside the tournament offices. John Paul is in awe. He quickly notices a large photo on the wall of Tiger holding the trophy from his previous win.

"That would look really cool on my wall," he states taking everything in.

Tiffany shows us around and then explains that we will go with the tournament director to the first tee and watch Tiger tee off. Then we can walk along with the crowd and watch him play. After the round we will meet Tiffany on the practice tee and hopefully at that time John Paul can meet Tiger.

We are ushered to the first tee to a special vantage point where we watch Tiger tee hit his first drive, and we begin our venture following his round. The crowds are astounding; it becomes hard to get a glimpse, so we walk a couple of holes ahead and wait at the greens. On the fifth green Tiger putts for birdie. John Paul stands by the ropes and claps. When Tiger exits the green he does something very unusual, he looks at John Paul and says, "Hey kid, think quick." Then he tosses John Paul his ball. The gallery cheers in awe, knowing that this is a rarity for Tiger.

The smile on John Paul's face as he turns to show me and his mom the ball is totally priceless.

"Thank goodness I caught it," he says admiring the ball. "Maybe you better put this in your pocketbook. I sure don't want to lose it," he says handing the ball to his mom.

We follow a bit longer until John Paul becomes tired, so we head to the eighteenth hole to wait. After the round the tournament manager and Tiffany lead John Paul to the media room where he watches Tiger answer questions. Afterwards John Paul waits outside hoping to meet the person he so admires. When Tiger exits the room he is introduced to John Paul. The compassion is clear as Tiger speaks to John Paul, allows pictures to be taken and even signs John Paul's cap and his collectibles.

John Paul takes great pride in his signed Tiger memorabilia. Much to his delight, this past Christmas he received a new collectors item. The package arrived a few days before Christmas,

Annette and I securely hide it away until Christmas day. I brought the present in after he opened all his gifts. His face showed the delight of having one more gift to open.

"What's this?" he questioned while ripping the paper off and discarding it to the floor. "Oh my goodness! Are you kidding me?" He pulled out the large picture of Tiger which had been on the wall at the Arnold Palmer Invitational.

"Can you believe it? This is the picture of when Tiger won the tournament!"

Annette walked over and lifted the picture so he could get a better view. "Tiffany remembered you saying you wanted the picture so, voilà!"

John Paul reached deeper into the box and retrieved a picture of him and Tiger. "Hey look at this! Tiger signed this picture of us!"

"You are one lucky boy, John Paul," I say patting him on the back.

"You're right dad. I am very lucky."

The Hospital–June 1997

The mundane atmosphere gnaws away at me, doctors and nurses chart information, take vitals, draw blood, yet the primary problem has not been addressed. I cannot let time slip by, each minute counts. I walk over to the desk and ask the nurse to page Dr. Harmon.

My son is a fighter; he has proved himself on more than one occasion. I stand and massage John Paul's leg; a smile etches across my face as I think about an incident. It has always been a chore getting John Paul to eat. I think back to a Sunday morning; we are at my parent's home and have just finished breakfast. I decide it is time for John Paul to eat his first egg. I place him in his highchair, mash the egg and do the entire pep talk routine. I watch his face; as soon as I scoop up a spoonful, he begins to shake his head no and holds up his hands to stop me.

"Here comes the airplane." I swirl my hand around and just as the plane full of egg is about to land it is suddenly diverted to the floor and a loud scream echoes throughout the room. John Paul is not happy. To this day I can still see his beet red face. Tears flow, but I gather more egg on the spoon.

"No dad, no egg!" his voice demands through the whimpers.

"John Paul, eggs are good for you." This time there is no airplane gliding in the sky, John Paul is too clever. Now the entire family is in the kitchen doing stunts to capture John Paul's attention. Somehow, I manage to get the spoonful of egg in his mouth. The element of surprise plastered on his face is priceless; however, his true willpower and fighter instincts reveal themselves. I watch in disbelief, he refuses to swallow the egg. Instead, he leaves his mouth wide open, holds the egg under his tongue, and cries.

"John Paul, swallow the egg."

He shakes his head no. For the next ten minutes, yes ten minutes, he holds his mouth open, the egg still in position. He is determined not to eat the egg. Finally, I concede, I cannot stand to see him cry; I take a napkin, clean the egg from his mouth, lift him out of his highchair and watch as he runs to play. I think of the good times, hoping they will pull me through the bad.

My thoughts are interrupted by a hand on my shoulder; I turn to face Dr. Harmon. The doctor and I step a few paces away from John Paul's bed.

"I can't help but think that if I suggest the smallest amount of dosage of blood thinner, maybe that will break up the clot." I look back at John Paul and continue, "but I have a conflicting thought; what if instead of breaking up the clot, the blood thinner releases the clot and causes a heart attack. Either way the odds are not in his favor, my son is caught in a catch twenty- two."

Dr. Harmon weighs the suggestion, but does not speak. He walks back over and looks at the latest labs.

"The labs have not improved, the liver enzymes continue to elevate, and urine output with the dialysis has not shown significant improvement. I have to tell you, if John Paul's liver enzymes do not decrease and his urine output does not increase the consequences will be fatal. I suggest a low dosage of Heparin, a blood thinner administered intravenously. At present this is our only option, there is no other viable alternative."

I look at my son, something has to be done, I can not stand around and hope things will work out. It does not happen that way. The odds are stacked against John Paul. Although he is a fighter he can't fight this battle alone, I have to help him.

With no other alternative, I give permission to start the drug. Within minutes, the nurse orders and administers the drug. Once again, Annette and I wait. As time progresses waiting does not get any easier, if anything it gets harder. I think about life and the amount of time spent waiting, waiting in traffic, at stoplights, in the grocery store, at the bank, at the doctor's office. Those trivial waits cannot compare to waiting for life or death results for a child, your child.

The first lab results since administering Heparin show no change, the liver count has not increased, but it has not decreased either. I tell myself this is a positive result and trust the next lab starts to show improvement.

The next lab result arrives late in the afternoon, the liver enzymes count has decreased and the urine output has increased slightly. The results confirm that the drug is dissolving the clot. I clutch Annette's hand tightly; finally, John Paul is heading in the right direction.

It is hard to believe, but the next few days are smooth sailing. From the deepest low to the highest high, I am on top of the world; my son is on the mend. I begin to see a light at the end of the tunnel. John Paul is slowly weaned out of his drug-induced coma and gradually becomes more aware of his surroundings.

Annette arrives from her makeshift sleeping quarters around six-thirty in the morning. She encourages me to go and get some rest. During our conversation, Dr. Harmon and residents arrive on their morning rounds. They examine John Paul, and discussion follows. The news is great! Today John Paul will be extubated (remove the ventilator) allowing him to begin breathing on his own, a huge step in the recovery process. Annette and I are anxious and thrilled. Time is not wasted; by eight in the morning the tube is removed, all that remains is a facial oxygen mask that covers John Paul's nose and mouth. The large protruding tube is gone! By ten o'clock, my little boy is sitting up in his bed and smiling. I am on top of the world! Feeling like a million bucks.

Annette's mom walks into PICU; John Paul gives a big wave, lifts the oxygen mask up and says, "Hey grandma!"

I am in awe, so is everyone in PICU. It is hard to believe this is the same little boy who just days ago was fighting for his life. I am relieved, but with the relief comes the realization that I am exhausted. Annette once again encourages me to go and get some rest, and finally I heed her advice.

From Annette:

To be honest, I am a nervous wreck when Derek leaves, although he is just down the hall, I am insecure when he is not with me. He can take control of a situation, I am not that assertive. Today is different though, John Paul looks great, he is sitting up and smiling, and I am at ease. I sit beside my mom, who is with me, and we talk to John Paul. He loves to hear stories about family members so I conjure up some funny tales of the past.

A young man enters, dressed like any other doctor, and informs me that he is going to change the Arterial Line. I watch him wash his hands, put gloves on and arrange the utensils for the procedure. I ask him to show me which line he is supposed to change. He points to the A-Line in the left side of John Paul's neck. I question the importance of changing the A-Line at this point. I explain that John Paul has only been extubated for a few hours and do not feel this should be done right now. Since the hospital is a teaching institute I ask the man if he is a resident or doctor. He does not appreciate the inquiry and states he is a resident in training. I question why a full pledge doctor is not doing this procedure. He assures me in no uncertain terms that he is fully capable of changing the line, and it will only take a few minutes. He then asks me to step outside until the procedure is complete. I am uneasy about the situation but adhere to his request. Before leaving, I advise him that John Paul is petrified of doctors and needles. I plead for him to take it easy and to stop if John Paul gets agitated because if he feels threatened he goes into turmoil. I kiss John Paul and tell him I will be back in few minutes.

My mom and I walk back to the waiting room. I look at my watch and notice twenty minutes have passed. I walk to the phone and call PICU, the nurse states the doctor is still working with John Paul. I am concerned, so without hesitation I slam the phone down and rush into PICU. At the entrance of the door, I hear my son heaving for air through each whimper of cry. Rounding the corner, I cannot believe my eyes, John Paul's head is dangling forward, his body limp with exhaustion. The resident is still probing at his neck.

"Make him stop!" I shout to the nurses sitting at the desk. I run up to John Paul's bed. "Stop it! You are going to kill him. Can't you see he is in distress?"

The resident notifies me that he knows what he is doing and has the situation under control. I cannot believe the smugness of this idiot!

When my mom and I left PICU, not even thirty minutes ago, John Paul was improving, smiling and happy. Now he is barely here and deteriorating fast. I cannot get anyone to listen to me. I make a mad dash out of PICU and run down the hall. I approach the room where Derek is sleeping, my body slams against the door and it bolts open.

"Derek!" My voice shrieks off the walls, at the sound of my cry Derek jumps up.

From Derek:

I walk into the room that has become my bedroom, close the blinds and get comfortable, as comfortable as one can get on a vinyl couch. A certain peace overcomes me, John Paul is doing better, finally I can rest. I fall into a deep sleep, suddenly I hear Annette screaming my name. I wake in horror, leap to my feet and try to figure out where I am. I see Annette at the door panicking. I do not even take time to ask her what is wrong, I flee past her, sprint down the hall, hit the automatic door opener and dash into PICU. *Dear God! What has happened?* John Paul is no longer sitting up in the bed smiling or waving. No, he is now lying down with teams of doctors and nurses surrounding him. I rush to the bed, when the nurse sees me she ask that I wait outside. Wait outside, I don't think so.

"What are they doing to him?"

"John Paul is being reintubated."

The response drills a hole in my stomach. In simple terms, the ventilator tube is being reinserted.

"Explain to me why the tube is being reinserted. When I went to lay down John Paul was doing fine without the ventilator. What happened?"

By this time Annette is at my side. She points to a person I have never seen before and tells me he tried to change the A-Line in John Paul's neck. He got John Paul into a state and would not stop, and now this is the result.

"I need Dr. Harmon paged immediately."

"Dr. Harmon is in surgery, Dr. Mays is covering."

"Then page Dr. Mays immediately!"

I stand and watch respiratory doctors attempt to stabilize my frail son. Annette stands near the door, the pressure is too much for her. She is nervous enough and this episode is pushing her close to the edge. I look at her, for the first time I notice how much weight she has lost, the hollowness of her eyes. I am not only worried for my son, but my wife also. I do not know what to do. Each time I think I see a glimmer of light at the end of the tunnel it is abruptly zapped out.

I am in a dust storm of doctors and nurses frantically whizzing around, doing everything possible to save John Paul. The resident who caused this atrocity is nonchalantly meandering around my son's bed. This irritates me immensely; I want him out of my sight, away from my son. Dr. Mays enters the room, stunned at the vision before him; he does not ask questions, he immediately takes control of the situation. Within fifteen minutes John Paul is reintubated, and back in a drug-induced coma. The image is a complete three-sixty from two hours ago. Even as I write this, all these years later, tears swell in my eyes as I think of all my young son has endured.

My emotions erupt; this situation could have been avoided. My son is at death's doors due to the stupidity of a reckless resident, who still hovers over my son.

"Get him out of here! I do not want him anywhere near my son," I tell Dr. Mays, pointing to the resident.

The doctor honors my request. I watch the resident, his head high, strut out of PICU. Dr. Mays, Annette and I enter a small conference, Annette and I sit on the end of the couch across from the doctor. The tension is thick. The doctor is nervous, and he should be. He knows the irresponsible actions of the resident can prompt a lawsuit. I begin the conversation.

"Negligence is the reason my son is fighting for his life. He was fine until the resident starting working on him. Annette explained to the resident that John Paul is afraid of doctors and needles and to take it easy and not get John Paul agitated, but he did not listen to the request, otherwise we would not be sitting here. From this day forward I do not want that resident or any other resident near my son."

The doctor understands my concern and affirms the resident will not be allowed to care for John Paul. He does, however, say that it being a teaching hospital, it will be hard not to have residents work with John Paul. I do not back down from my position, I reinforce my wish that however hard it may be, no residents or interns are to work on my son.

This medical mistake extended John Paul's hospital stay by a month, but more importantly, almost cost him his life.

In reference to the changing or inserting an Arterial Line, The Internet Journal of Health states:

This is a very safe procedure, performed by highly trained professionals.

The Internet Journal of Health ™ ISSN: 1528-8315

My wish is a highly trained professional would have performed my son's procedure.

Chapter Eleven

Love

"Where there is great love, there are always miracles."

Willa Cather

Glen is a gentleman who lived in our neighborhood. He constantly prayed for John Paul. During John Paul's third stage of surgery and hospital stay, Annette's family kept him updated on John Paul's condition; however, he became ill and entered intensive care at the local hospital. The doctors did not think he would make it. His wife said he prayed fervently that God would take his life and spare John Paul. God spared both lives, yet a couple of years later Glen passed on. It wasn't until after his passing that we became aware of his plead to God. To this day I am in awe that someone unrelated to John Paul could have such unconditional love that he would be willing to give his own life for my son.

John Paul and Chris Tucker

Fall 2003

Excitement fills the air. John Paul can hardly contain himself; a smile has been on his face since he got the news. It is nice when people follow through on promises made, especially promises made to a child.

A few years ago John Paul and Annette had tickets to a sneak preview at the Muvico at City Place in downtown West Palm Beach. I am in New York on a business trip, so they decide to make an evening of it and stop at the Cheesecake Factory for dinner. Annette tells the story. The restaurant is in a bustle; Michael Jackson just left, quite a star sighting for the area. John Paul questions the waiter who happily fills him in on the scoop.

"By the way, I hear Chris Tucker from Rush Hour is also at City Place," the waiter tells John Paul.

This sends John Paul over the top. Michael Jackson is the king of pop, but John Paul is a movie buff and an avid fan of Chris Tucker and the Rush Hour movies.

"Where is he?" his voice shrieks with enthusiasm.

The waiter tells John Paul he heard Chris Tucker is at the movie theater. Normally a slow eater, John Paul gobbles his food and exclaims he is ready to go to the movie. The waiter brings the bill and an update, Michael Jackson is at Barnes and Noble.

"John Paul, we have to go to Barnes and Noble, this is a once in a lifetime chance to meet Michael Jackson."

"Mom, I want to go to see Chris Tucker."

"We still have plenty of time, let's go quickly and see if you can see Michael Jackson, from there we will go directly to the movie theater."

Reluctantly he agrees. At Barnes and Noble, the music section is closed, allowing Michael Jackson to shop alone. John Paul is now thrilled and wants to meet him. One thing about John Paul, he is not shy. He sneaks in and goes directly up to Michael Jackson and says, "Excuse me do you have the Pearl Harbor video?"

Michael Jackson is dumbfounded. He looks at his bodyguard and laughs.

"The kid thinks I work here."

The bodyguard comes over and starts to escort John Paul out, but Michael Jackson stops him. He proceeds to scan the store, with John Paul at his side, looking for Pearl Harbor. When he finds it, he hands it to John Paul and the two walk over toward me. He asks John Paul something, I see my son point to me. Michael Jackson motions for me to come to him.

"Your son wants this Pearl Harbor video."

Now I am the one dumbfounded. I graciously thank him for helping John Paul and ask for an autograph. I search through my purse, all I can find is my Cheesecake Factory receipt and my eyeliner pencil. I hand them both to him, he laughs.

"You want me to sign with an eyeliner pencil?"

By now the crowd who gathered around the music section notices he is signing autographs and start pushing their way toward Michael Jackson handing him things to sign. He uses the eyeliner pencil to sign, smiles at John Paul as he hands it back to me, the bodyguard moves him through the crowd, and we watch as he exits the store.

"Come mom, we got to hurry; we got to get to the movie theater."

At the theater the attendant explains that the movie is full and no one else is allowed in. Needless to say my son is disappointed. The attendant overhears John Paul say he wants to meet Chris Tucker. He informs us that Chris Tucker is in the movie we were supposed to see. That is all John Paul needs to hear, he decides we must sit and wait. We park ourselves on the bench and wait. Thirty minutes pass, forty-five minutes pass.

"John Paul it is getting late, the movie will not be out for another forty-five minutes, we really need to go. You already met Michael Jackson."

"Please mom, just five more minutes. I want to see Chris Tucker."

Call it fate, destiny, whatever you want, but just as we start to leave I see this gentleman walk out of the theater.

"Mom, that is Chris Tucker!"

I watch my son scurry and call, "Chris Tucker!"

The tall man turns around and catches a glimpse of John Paul and smiles.

"Hey there little man."

The two carry on a conversation for ten minutes talking about Rush Hour. He is amazed John Paul knows all his one-liners. John Paul asks for his autograph, when he can't find anything for him to sign, John Paul points to his new white Air Jordan's. Chris Tucker, who thankfully has his own pen, gets down on his hands and knees and sign my son's shoes, *Love, Chris Tucker.*

I thank him for being so nice, and explain a little about John Paul's condition. He takes out a card, writes his home number and his agent's home number on it and looks at John Paul.

"I want you to come to my next movie premier. Your mom has my numbers; we'll stay in touch."

John Paul's eyes light up, he gives Chris a hug and thanks him.

As we start to walk away John Paul turns and adds one more commentary, "By the way, you need to get a new partner, Jackie Chan is getting too old."

"Who do you think my new partner should be?"

John Paul does a karate move and smiles. "Me!"

August 2007

The eight hour drive to Atlanta seems like sixteen to John Paul, but we finally arrive, the big day is here. He precisely places his clothes on the bed and goes to shower. Derek and I laugh at how long it takes him, but we let him absorb every minute of the thrill. Once at the theater, Derek saves our seats while John Paul and I wait in the lobby for Chris Tucker. John Paul spots him first, and dashes straight for him. Tears build as I watch my son beam as Chris Tucker bends down to greet him. His agent and bodyguards try to get him to hurry, but he ignores them. His focus is on my son. The two reminisce about their last meeting at a movie house and he tells John Paul he wants him to meet his son after the premier. We follow Chris into the theater and watch a VIP screening of Rush Hour 3.

It is amazing, Chris Tucker followed through on a promise made four years prior, impressive for someone of his stature. His simple act of kindness showered blessings and uplifted my son.

Back at the hospital June 1997...

The hospital administrative personnel suddenly surround my family constantly. Our every need is now top priority; unfortunately this is not out of compassion or kindness, rather out of fear. The hospital realizes that the mistake of the resident almost cost John Paul his life and unnecessarily increased his hospital stay. Fear encourages their acts of kindness, fear of a lawsuit. Annette and I contemplate the lawsuit issue, but we push it aside. We are grateful; God has been good to us, spared our son and we do not feel the added pressure of a lawsuit would be beneficial.

Per my request John Paul is moved to a private room in PICU. The night brings a fragment of stability. Annette and I have been at the hospital since the surgery. I refuse to go to the Ronald McDonald House directly across the street. I can't leave the building, even if it is just across the street, that's too far, my place is with my son. Annette and I take shifts; I take the night, and she takes the day. The social worker and administrator have given up their endeavor of steering us to the Ronald McDonald House; they realize their request is futile. The administrator offers a room at the end of the ICU hall, a storage area for chairs with one vinyl couch; it's not much, but it serves the purpose. I send Annette to her makeshift sleeping quarters, the day has been horrendous, stress is beginning to take its toll on her. I am not only concerned for my son; I also worry for the well-being of my wife.

I dim the lights on John Paul's bed and sit down in the chair next to him. I think about the past three years. I rehash the good times, his first word; unfortunately it wasn't dad but rather Bo, the name of our neighbor's Golden Retriever, who everyday arrived at our sliding glass door to visit John Paul. His first birthday party, the first time he saw Mickey Mouse, his first Christmas. I smile at the happy thoughts; however the events of the day chase away my positive feelings. In the early morning hours, I played the role of a puppet in a play, but soon realize to save my son I must be the puppeteer. John Paul's condition was deteriorating and the doctors were dumfounded. If I hadn't pleaded to the doctor to scan the liver the clot never would have been detected. I assertively instructed the doctors and residents to search the internet for treatment options. It scares me, blood thinner being the only resolution available to try to dissolve the clot in John Paul's liver. A blood thinner after heart surgery is a fatal drug, but so is a blood clot, as a result my son is in a catch twenty-two. One simple mishap and John Paul can bleed to death. The thick anxiety and atmosphere makes me feel like I have aged twenty years in one day. My body is drained physically, mentally, and emotionally, yet I know I must persevere for the sake of my son.

I am not sure of the time, I know it's late, there's not much movement in NICU. I use the down time to try to settle my nerves. I pick up the cassette tapes from the table, UB40, James Taylor, Elton John, the Beatles, and the Bee Gees. I insert the Bee Gees into the tape player and place it beside John Paul's bed so he is able to hear it. The soothing sound relaxes me; finally, I feel a sense of calmness. I flip through a magazine, the tape stops; I reach up and turn it over to the other side and hit play. A respiratory therapist walks toward the door and enters. It is not the regular therapist, Mike, but someone I have not met before. It has been a long day and since the suctioning routine usually does not affect John Paul, I do not bother getting up to greet her.

The young woman is dressed in the royal blue respiratory attire; her dark hair is tightly secured in a ponytail. I say hello and inform her that John Paul is on a blood thinner. I am precise in my explanation not knowing if she has been briefed on my son's condition. I have learned to never assume the assumed.

She walks over to the sink, loads her palms with soap, washes her hands and dries them thoroughly. She hums along with the music while meticulously arranging her utensils in preparation for the procedure. I watch her slowly insert the tube down through John Paul's nose with care, then I lean my head on the back of the chair, close my eyes and meditate.

All of a sudden, a shrill reverberates within the room. My eyes jolt wide open, my body thrusts to the edge of the chair. Total disbelief shakes my world; I can't believe what is happening in front of me. Everything seems to be in slow motion. I watch as blood travels up the tube and spews out John Paul's nose. *This can't be!* My emotions twirl into a tailspin, my body is in a state of shock. The therapist doesn't know what to do. She continues to push the tube further down, suctioning, agitating the situation. She will not stop.

I leap to my feet. "What are you doing?"

Instead of removing the tube, she frantically continues to suction and jab deeper.

"Take it easy!"

The words barely have time to depart my lips; suddenly a gush of blood erupts out of the tube. I watch my son's blood splatter toward the wall and floor. The crisp white bed linens are infused with blemishes of crimson. The therapist's face is pallid white and laced with speckles of blood, her hands shudder uncontrollably, the blood continues to surge all over the therapist and onto floor. She grasps the tube tighter, her eyes rapidly searching around ICU for help, no one is in sight. Her voice bellows in vain for anyone, there is no response. My insides feel like I am being thrust into the cockpit of Jumbo 747 that is spiraling out of control.

"We're losing him!" she cries out.

I don't know what to do, my nerves are completely shattered. I glare out to the hallway; no doctor or nurse are in sight. I turn back to face more horror, blood begins to seep out of John Paul's mouth.

Please someone shake me, wake me from this nightmare, I can't take it anymore! I'm watching my son bleed to death.

A cyclone is speeding through every inch of my body, and then out of nowhere a warm sensation filters through me, the same warmth I experienced three years earlier. I feel calmness, a sudden sense of control.

I move to the therapist, place my hand on her arm, my touch brings us face to face. Her bloodshot eyes are hollow, unsure of what to do.

"Calm down, everything's gonna be alright. Slowly pull the tube out." I listen to the words exit my mouth, yet I am unsure of where they are coming from.

She feels the calmness, and slowly her shaking hands retract the tube. I tighten my hand around her arm and ask her to back off hoping the bleeding will stop. Side by side we stand, scared senseless, holding our breath. I hear nothing except the loud beat of my heart which thumps hard against my chest. I am in a time capsule, minutes seem like hours, but then it happens, the bleeding subsides. I can't believe my eyes, my emotions are spent, I exhale relief with the last bit of breath in me. Tears stream down the therapist's face, her bottom lip quivers; she attempts to speak but is unable to.

The NICU doctor rushes from another patient's bedside into the room, he stops and takes notice of what looks like a war zone. Winded from the ordeal, I can barely talk; the therapist gains her composure and gives details of the ordeal as the doctor begins to attend to John Paul. I walk over to the sink, wet a cloth and wipe the blood from John Paul's mouth and swollen face. The therapist pulls off numerous paper towels from the dispenser, wets them, then gets down on her hands and knees and begins cleaning the blood from the floor. I stumble away from the bed, my legs buckle; I drop to my knees, and help her clean up my son's blood.

After everyone leaves the room, I sit on the edge of John Paul's bed. Something miraculous just happened. Just like it happened three years prior in the wee hours of the morning after John Paul's first surgery when we almost lost him. Another miracle. How else can it be explained? There is no other explanation as to how the bleeding stopped. I notice the blood stains on my clothes, even though I have washed my hands there are still remnants of blood under my nails. I look at John Paul, oblivious to the chaos. My eyes scan the ventilator tube protruding from his small mouth. His body remains still as a statue from the drug-induced coma. I cannot believe this little boy's fate, there is an obstacle at every turn. Not even a few hours can pass without a jolt of uncertainty striking. I am shattered, not for myself but for my son and upset that his fight for life is made more complicated by ridiculous errors. The third stage, the final stage of the Norwood Procedure, posed more complications than one ever could have imagined. **I have to wonder will he remember all he has endured, the trauma? Will it affect his life, his dreams?**

John Paul is finally extubated and after weeks of being in PICU he is moved to the pediatric floor. The drugs have been tapered, and he is awake after being in a drug-induced coma for three weeks. His body and muscles are weak; he resembles a Raggedy Anne doll. I prop pillows around him so he can sit up. He sits in a daze most of the day, he is not the same little boy, he is void of any expression. I turn the television to his favorite show, but he stares blankly into space. I am worried and begin to wonder if there has been brain damage, but I keep this thought to myself.

I tell jokes, dance, and sing anything to boost John Paul's morale; however, the response is the same. I rack my brain thinking of things to lift his spirit. He loves the outdoors. I speak to the doctor and make arrangements to take him outside once or twice a day. Annette and I prop him up in his stroller and walk around outside. We walk around the gardens, up and down the sidewalks. Sometimes we sit under shade trees and let him absorb the fresh air, but most of the time he sleeps. I hope being outside, feeling the heat of the sunlight, the flutter of the breeze, the chirp of the birds and the noises of everyday life will help him heal.

Nighttime is the worst. Panicky screams pierce the darkness. Annette and I jump out of the hospital chair that has become our makeshift bed. I turn on the light above John Paul's bed. His screams intensify, his legs kick and arms wave erratically in front of him. This is not the first night this has happened, it has become a routine occurrence. Every night around one or two it starts. It is terrifying, he cries nonstop. I do not know what is causing him to do this, even the nurses can not offer an explanation. Is it nightmares? Nightmares about all he has endured? There is no way to know, all I can do is try to pacify him. Annette and I both try holding him, comforting him, singing to him, nothing works. Finally we put him in his stroller and roam the halls of the pedantic ward for two to three hours, and for some reason this calms him. As soon as the stroller stops he begins to scream. I try to figure out why the stroller ride is calming. I remember Annette placing John Paul in his stroller as a baby and pushing him around until he fell asleep. Maybe he reverts back to his infancy and the movement of the stroller comforts him. It is only later as I read the nursing notes that I find out the cause of the hysteria.

PICU Notes
Patient: John Paul George
MR # 1171909

Of note this morning John Paul appeared agitated and was thought by nurse to hallucinate. It is unclear to me whether this represents with-

drawal symptoms vs. residual ketamine metabolites vs. a drug reaction or possibly CNS impairment due to venous or air emboli around the time of his cardiac surgery.

Withdrawal, drugs or a central nervous system impairment caused by an air pocket in a vein was never discussed. When asked the cause of these nighttime episodes the staff is baffled, or that is the reaction portrayed. No one ever explained these issues or the side effects of the high-power narcotics administered to John Paul, but we later find out.

For the last two months he has been receiving nutrition intravenously, some of the simple tasks learned have to be reintroduced, such as learning to sip. Annette and I were criticized greatly by friends for giving John Paul Coke and Sprite at the age of two and three, but we had our reasons. The two soft drinks, loaded with calories, helped put weight on John Paul and built him up for the third surgery. I know how much John Paul loves Sprite; I take a straw and squirt a little in his mouth. His taste buds ignite, and I watch with delight as he smacks his lips together and motions for more. Slowly he is reunited with some of his favorite foods. I feel better as he begins to eat because I know with each bite he will begin to get his strength back.

Dr. Harmon stops by to visit and check on John Paul. He begins the conversation by asking about John Paul's intake. This is important, at every doctor visit the first question has always been an inquiry into John Paul's intake. If he is eating, his body can thrive and heal. I happily report John Paul has been eating better with each passing day. The doctor is pleased, but then says something that blindsides both Annette and I.

"From this point forward, John Paul cannot have salt."

I ask if he said low salt or no salt. He clarifies no salt and states he will have a dietician come by and speak to Annette and me about a healthy diet for John Paul. Wow, I think about no salt, almost absolutely everything has salt, bread, milk, cheese, not to mention the things most kids love, chips, chicken nuggets and McDonalds hamburgers. I have to wonder, what is my son going to eat? He needs his nutrition. This day marks the beginning of a never-ending obstacle, one that becomes more difficult with time.

The discharge day is in sight, only one more hurdle to clear, the issue of how to administer a blood thinner at home. While in the hospital the Heparin given to break up the clot in the liver and prevent future clots has been administered intravenously. The challenge is to find a drug which can be given to John Paul at home. Most blood thinners are geared toward the older generation. The doctor states the only option is to give John Paul Coumadin, a high-powered blood thinner. Dr. Harmon explains we will have to monitor the thickness of John Paul's blood daily. I can't imagine how I am going to monitor the thickness of his blood daily. It's hard to fathom taking him each day for blood work. I know how petrified he is of needles, the thought of him having to be pricked daily makes me sick to my stomach. The doctor's next sentence shrills me to the bone. *You will monitor his blood at home.*

I picture what his words mean, me, not a nurse, getting blood samples daily. I have seen how he panics, works himself into a state when a nurse attempts to draw blood, now I will be the one who pricks John Paul. I am shell-shocked. I thought inserting a feeding tube when he was a baby was bad; this is different, John Paul is older, aware of what is going on. I cannot comprehend what this will do to him; he will hate me, never forgive me, and lose all faith in me.

Catching up with the conversation, I hear the doctor say a coagulation monitor will need to be purchased. The monitor determines the clotting time of John Paul's blood, which is extremely important. Coumadin, the drug being prescribed, is an adult drug, not meant for children; therefore John Paul will have to be watched closely to make sure his blood does not get too thin. If that happens something as simple as a sneeze can cause internal bleeding. The bleeding is deadly because it can go undetected and not be discovered until it is too late.

"There has to be something else we can give John Paul, this drug seems too strong," I say thinking out loud.

Dr. Harmon reiterates Coumadin is the only solution and that everything should be fine, as long as we monitor the results closely. He leaves an information brochure on the monitor and states he will have one available tomorrow.

The joy of John Paul being discharged escapes, I cannot stop thinking about the task that will have to performed at home. I will do anything for my son and if this is what it takes to get him out of this hospital and home, then so be it. We will work through this just as we have worked through everything else.

Nursing Notes:
7/25/97
9:50 am
See discharge sheet for summary and specific instructions and mother verbalized to nurse her complete understanding of all instructions. Patient discharged via father's arms for home.

Chapter Twelve

Peace

If we have no peace, it is because we have forgotten that we belong to each other.

Mother Teresa

John Paul and the U.S. Navy

September 2007

The old saying, time heals all wounds, is true. Not only does time heal wounds but for me it produces complacency. For the last few years John Paul has been fortunate, sickness has stayed out of his path allowing me to become relaxed in the daily routine of life. However, Friday night jolts me back to reality.

Eight years ago we started a tradition in our house, Friday night is movie night. This is John Paul's night. He chooses the restaurant for dinner and movie he wants to see. He looks forward to this night the entire week. As soon as I retrieve the morning paper he is gazing at the movie section planning his evening. This Friday night is no different; we go out for dinner and go see a movie he has been waiting months to see. One thing unique about John Paul is his laugh, it is pure, deep from his stomach and highly contagious. A friend said if he could only bottle John Paul's laugh he would be a millionaire. I cannot say the movie is funny, but I laugh. I laugh with my son who is thoroughly enjoying the comedy.

Afterwards, I hurry home to finish packing for an early flight in the morning. I am uneasy, as I am anytime I have to leave, but more so tonight because I will have to be gone for a week. Once home John Paul gets ready for bed. I hear him tell his mom he does not feel well, and then I hear his feet scurry across the floor as he runs into the bathroom. The next sound is disturbing, a long gag, and then the release of food into the toilet bowl. Annette is already by his side, I rush in and watch more food hurl from his mouth. Annette takes a cool cloth, wipes his face and I help him back to his bed. He says he feels better, so I go back to packing while Annette sits with him. I am relieved he feels better but my relief is short-lived. Within twenty minutes he is back in the bathroom repeating the earlier scene. After the fourth time I get anxious because of all he has been through, with the distended stomach and protein loss. My thoughts swirl. Does he have a stomach virus? Does he have food poisoning? What if there is a problem in his abdomen?

The pain intensifies instead of getting better with the release of the food. I carry him and place him in our bed. He jumps up and does not make it to the bathroom before more food comes up. His face is beet red, his body limp from exhaustion, I carry him back to the bed. Annette lies beside him, I lay at the foot of the bed, and we watch him. He falls asleep, but the pain grips him; again he is out of the bed, but this time phlegm expels from his mouth and the dry heaves begin. My anxiety intensifies. John Paul falls asleep again. Annette and I walk into the dining room, sit at the table and stare blankly at the cityscape lights. Tonight I return to reality after a hiatus. John Paul is delicate, sometimes I forget. Memories of past worrisome nights, the present unknown churns my stomach. Annette and I realize we may have to take John Paul to the hospital if this does not resolve.

John Paul is up again, this time fatigue will not allow him out of the bed, what little is left in him dispenses onto the bed. Afterwards his head drops to the pillow, his eyes flutter and shut. I have to get liquids in his body before dehydration settles in. I take the gas out of ginger ale, wake him, get him to take a sip and let him go back to sleep. All three of us lay on the bed. Every time his body moves Annette and I both jerk up to make sure he is okay. Finally an hour passes without him being sick, I hold my breath, another hour passes, then at three o'clock I doze off. I wake at four forty-five, John Paul is feeling better which makes me feel like a million bucks.

Tonight's ordeal triggered a visitation to a time locked in the recesses of my mind. It reminded me that every day, every hour with John Paul is a blessing and not one minute should be taken for granted.

July 1997

I have experienced many different feelings and emotions, but the one I feel now is indescribable. John Paul is out of the hospital, all three stages of the Norwood Procedure complete. At last I can breathe. A weight the size of Texas has been lifted from my shoulders.

We will be in North Carolina for two weeks until John Paul goes back for his post operation check-up. The mood in Annette's parents' home, where we are staying, is jubilant. John Paul is home! I hope being in a familiar environment will encourage healing and I will begin to see hints of the John Paul before surgery. Unfortunately, the night terrors continue, as does the nonresponsiveness. He is not completely unresponsive; he begins to talk more with each passing day, but something still is not right. Annette and I sit on the front porch swing, John Paul sits on Annette's lap. My niece, Leigh Ann, who John Paul calls La, walks onto the porch. I put my finger to my lip and motion for her to keep quiet.

"John Paul, who just walked outside?"

He does not answer right away, finally he says, "Grandma."

Annette and I look at each other. I stand up in front of him and Annette asks.

"John Paul, who is standing in front of you?"

"Kia," Kia, his nickname for his Aunt Cecilia.

The air is vacuumed from my lungs, I can no longer breathe. Annette shakes her head and mouths. *He can't see!* I think of all he has been through in the last two months, open-heart surgery, a second surgery for bleeding, clot in his liver, kidney failure, loss of circulation in his leg, near-death experience from the resident and now I discover he is blind. I shake my head in disbelief and try not to let my emotions get the best of me. I go inside and call John, my friend who is a doctor. He has a way of calming my nerves and today is no different. I describe John Paul's symptoms. He tells me that several years ago his wife was on painkillers for MS for an extended period of time. When she stopped the drugs she could not see. This blindness was temporary, within two weeks she regained her sight. This makes me feel better. I know John Paul has been on high-powered painkillers and more than likely his blindness is a side effect from the drugs, but only time will tell.

A few days pass. It is five o'clock in the morning, I hear John Paul call. Annette gets up and the two of them go into the family room. I hear muffled sounds of the television; slowly I get out of bed and walk into the room. John Paul is sitting on Annette's lap. A balloon is floating beside the television. I pull on the ribbon attached to the balloon and out of nowhere John Paul says, "Tigger!"

I look at the television, Barney, not Winnie the Pooh is on. I glance at Annette her mouth is open in awe.

"Derek, look at the balloon, it is Tigger the tiger from Winnie the Pooh!"

"John Paul, who is holding the balloon?" Annette asks.

"Daddy!"

Annette and I squeeze John Paul tightly, our happiness can not be contained. We run up and down the hall waking the entire family and share the good news.

John Paul begins to transform into the little boy he was before the surgery. He passes his two week check-up with flying colors. There is only one drawback, I have to start checking John Paul's blood next week, a deed I dread.

The drive back to Florida is a complete three-sixty from the drive up to North Carolina. I remember the fear and anxiety I experienced driving up for John Paul's surgery. I was frightened my son would not be with me on my return trip. I look in the rearview mirror at my son sitting in the backseat. His brown eyes sparkle as our eyes meet. I silently thank God he is still with me.

The weeks that follow start off positive, but the only draw-back remains testing John Paul's blood. The repetitiveness does not lessen his anxiety. His reaction is the same every time he sees the needle, sheer fear. Today, the result shows his blood is too thin. I call the pediatric cardiologist in North Carolina and ask if I should reduce the dosage of Coumadin. The answer is no, stick to the same dosage because sometimes the readings fluctuate. I follow the instructions.

John Paul sits in his stroller and plays with his cousin, Leigh-Ann. Suddenly he becomes irritated for no reason, he shouts, his face turns blood red. I am flabbergasted, I have never seen him like this. He tells me he is tired and wants to lay down. I take him out of his stroller and place him on the bed. He falls asleep quickly. I tell myself exhaustion is the reason for his erratic behavior. I check on him throughout the afternoon. Finally, three hours later, he wakes up. He stays awake only momentarily before falling back to sleep. At five-thirty I wake John Paul and attempt to feed him, he is so drowsy that he cannot even chew the food. I take him back upstairs and lay him on the bed, within minutes he is back asleep. Annette and I stay in the room and watch him sleep, both of us anxious. Eight o'clock John Paul is still sleeping, I try to wake him, it takes me several times to finally rouse him. This is not normal, so Annette and I decide to take John Paul to the emergency room.

The three of us enter the emergency room, John Paul limp in my arms. The cardiologist on call enters the small room where we wait. I inform her that John Paul has Hypoplastic Left Heart and has recently had his third stage of surgery. She remarks that she has never seen a Hypoplastic Left Heart child and is fascinated with my son. I remind her why John Paul is at the emergency room and ask what could be the cause of the sleepiness. The doctor begins to examine John Paul, she panics when his saturations appear on the monitor. I advise her that the cardiologist in North Carolina told me to always look at John Paul, not the number, and as far as his coloring John Paul looks great. The low saturations bothers her, she struggles to gather her composure on that issue, but finally focuses on the reason John Paul is in the ER.

A virus is the diagnosis. The treatment, take him home, let him rest and he should be better in a day or two. Annette and I follow her directives and take our son back home. John Paul sleeps through the night and most of the next day. Late afternoon he wakes long enough to eat a small amount of food and then goes back to sleep. The next morning I wake around six, John Paul has not moved the entire night. I notice his body twitching, jerking abnormally. I am unable to wake him. I call my friend John, his advice is to get John Paul to the emergency room as soon as possible.

I ride in the ambulance with John Paul, Annette follows in the car behind us. I stand out of the way as John Paul is rushed into the emergency room. Annette and I are greeted by a young doctor who asks questions about John Paul's symptoms. I explain John Paul was at this hospital the night before and give a detailed account of what has been occurring. Annette and I stand by John Paul's bed. I watch Annette stroke his hair and whisper she loves him in his ear. The room is similar to the NICU at the hospital in North Carolina. I can't believe John Paul is back in this setting. When I left North Carolina I thought the hospital was a memory of the past, now this.

The doctor documents John Paul's chart and assures me my son is in good hands. Suddenly John Paul begins to have another seizure-like episode. The doctor observes the ordeal, within a minute or so the episode is over. I inform the doctor that the seizures started this morning and have become more frequent. The doctor does not hesitate. John Paul is immediately rushed to x-ray. Annette and I pace the emergency room corridor, nerves shattered, wondering what could be wrong.

The doctor, a young lady helping out from a top hospital in Miami, accompanies John Paul back to his room from the x-ray lab. She motions Annette and me to the corner of the room, her smile from earlier is evaporated.

"The reason John Paul has been sleeping so much and started having seizures is due to a brain hemorrhage." She pauses to let us absorb her words.

All of a sudden I feel out of my comfort zone. I am not in North Carolina where the doctors and nurses know John Paul, I am twelve hours away. What in the world am I going to do? I do not know anything about this hospital.

She continues on, "The hemorrhage is severe. I am afraid there is not much time."

"What do you mean not much time?"

"It is imperative that we get him to surgery immediately in order to release the pressure from the brain, otherwise John Paul will die."

I will not tolerate the word die, that word is void from my vocabulary.

"Can we chopper him to Miami?"

"There is not enough time. I have placed a call to the best neurosurgeon on staff, he is not on call, but the staff is trying to locate him." She receives a page and excuses herself.

Annette is emotionally distraught. She is frightened that this facility will not be able to handle John Paul and the severity of his condition. I watch her go to a phone, dial a number and plead to speak to Dr. Harmon. She tells Dr. Harmon the news, tears stream down her face, the phone trembles in her hand and after a few minutes she hangs up the phone.

"What did he say?"

"Dr. Harmon told me since we live in Florida we must establish our life-line here. We must trust the doctors and their ability. He also told me he will keep the lines open so the doctor can call him with any questions."

My parents and family arrive at the hospital. They have called relatives and friends to start the prayer chain. I watch Annette call her parents in North Carolina, an emotional conversation commences after hanging up; she tearfully tells me they are on their way down.

I feel a slight touch on my shoulder I turn to face the doctor.

"The neurosurgeon has been contacted, he should be here any minute. We are getting John Paul ready for surgery."

Annette and I go to our child's bedside. Once again, like many times before, our son is in need of a miracle, the odds are not in his favor. Annette does not stop kissing him and whispering words in his ear. She is no longer crying, she is strong and determined to transmit that demeanor to our son. I stand, watch and silently pray for another miracle.

The emergency room doctor informs us it is time to go. Annette and I accompany John Paul to the operating room. I cannot take my eyes off of him. I absorb his features, long dark eyelashes, full pink lips, smooth skin and long dark hair. In the recesses of my mind I hear his sweet innocent voice, his laughter, my body yearns to hear those sounds again. The walk is lengthy, and while on the way, John Paul is gripped with another seizure; our steps hasten. At the entrance of the operating room, the doctor and nurses pause briefly allowing us to kiss our son. I watch, as I have many times before, my son disappear to the unknown.

The waiting room consists of ten plastic chairs and a view of a lovely garden and statues. An elderly lady dressed in pink sits at a wooden desk. She is a volunteer who updates families on the status of surgery. Annette and I pace up and down in front of the windows, stopping every few minutes to look outside. I am shocked when the volunteer states the surgery is over and the doctor will be out soon. I fear the worst.

I see a tall man in blue scrub attire walking down the hallway. A million butterflies flutter in my stomach. Annette grabs my arm tightly, we both stand, the doctor approaches. Before he introduces himself he relieves our fears.

"John Paul is fine."

Annette and I break down, tears expel uncontrollably, another prayer answered, another miracle delivered.

The doctor introduces himself and proceeds to tell Annette and I about the surgery. A few minutes were the difference between life and death for John Paul. The doctor's face grows pale, he explains as soon as he drilled a hole in John Paul's skull the pressure from within released and blood gushed and spattered on the wall. Slight hesitation would have cost John Paul his life. I still get chills today when I think of what could have been.

The cause of the hemorrhage: John Paul's blood had become too thin from the Coumadin. I told the doctors up north the reading from his blood test, but they told me to keep the same dosage, which could have cost John Paul his life. Something as simple as a sneeze could have triggered the bleeding. The doctor's bewilderment was apparent, this life-threatening event could have been avoided. A simple baby aspirin should have been prescribed instead of the high-powered adult drug.

John Paul's hospital stay lasted several weeks. During that time a new life-line was established with his new pediatric cardiologist, Dr. Bowen and the nurses of the community.

The brain surgery did rob John Paul of one of his famous attributes, his long locks. However for more than a year after the surgery I made my son wear a bright yellow bumble bee helmet. I was not taking any chances, and the helmet became his trademark, that is, until his hair grew back out.

Physically, emotionally and mentally, the summer has been a series of catastrophic hurricanes: surviving landfall, a brief relaxation during the calm of the eye and then bracing again for the outer, more powerful wall. My only hope, this is it, the end of a turbulent season.

Chapter Thirteen

Pain

One word frees us of all the weight and pain of life: that word is love.

Sophocles

John Paul in the sand

There is no greater pain than seeing your child or loved one suffer, to me that is the ultimate pain. During the past years my family has experienced many different types of pain, but pain inflicted by others is a hard pain to bear.

I have a handicap sticker. I would much rather have a healthy child than the disability that affords me the right to have the sticker. I am used to "the looks" received from people who stare when John Paul and I get out of the car. Outward appearances can be deceiving and it is important to remember a person does not have to be in a wheelchair to be disabled.

Friday night Annette, John Paul and I go to our favorite pizza restaurant. I drop Annette at the front to get a seat while John Paul and I park the car. There is a lady sitting outside the restaurant. She watches me park in the handicap space. When we walk by she mumbles something. I ignore her, unsure of who she is speaking to. Then she speaks louder, others turn and take notice at the sound of her voice, "You need to move your ca;, you are not handicapped."

I cannot believe she is speaking to me. "Excuse me?"

"Everyone can clearly see you are not handicapped so you need to move your car."

John Paul tugs at my arm. "Daddy, what's wrong?"

I do not want John Paul to get upset, I tell him not to worry, everything is fine. The lady's villainous attitude is relentless. She continues harassing. John Paul grips my hand tightly and uses my body as a barrier.

"Why is she mad at us?" His bottom lip begins to quiver.

Now I am mad, an ignorant and meddlesome lady has upset my son. I open the restaurant door and let John Paul in. I turn and walk over to the lady.

"I would appreciate it if you would kindly mind your own business."

Everyone standing outside is eavesdropping on the conversation, even the people inside have started to take notice. I speak so everyone can hear. I do not want any further confusion about "the handicap sticker," plus a little education may help others who hastily draw conclusions before knowing the facts.

"A handicap is not always something that is visual. A person can be handicapped without being in a wheelchair or walking with a cane. I have a handicap sticker because my son has a serious heart problem. Trust me, I would much rather have a healthy child than a sticker that affords me special parking privileges. You should consider others' feelings and think before you speak."

The lady huffs. She could care less, she is void of any remorse for her actions. She sits and vicariously puffs away on her cigarette.

Needless emotional pain was inflicted on my family that night. For days John Paul inquired why the lady was so mean. That's a hard question to answer.

Summer 2000

The latest ordeal begins as John Paul approaches school age. I bet nine out of ten people tell me the same thing. *It is important for John Paul to go to school, to interact with children his own age.* This statement begins to play on my mind. Am I wrong for sheltering him in order to keep him healthy? Am I doing more harm than good? Sure, I am overprotective, but shouldn't I be? I think of the consequences. My niece and nephew come home from school with sore throats, colds, stomach viruses and the flu. The common cold can put John Paul in the hospital and the flu can be deadly. However I do not want to deprive my son of a full life, of childhood experiences.

I wish I would have followed my instincts; however, I did not. Annette and I enroll John Paul in a private kindergarten with only seven children in his class. He begins in August, and by the middle of September, he has bronchitis. He is out of kindergarten for weeks, his condition does not improve, it deteriorates. The pediatrician places him on steroids, antibiotics and breathing treatments.

One evening I am in the room with him, he is changing into his pajamas. I notice his stomach is distended. I call the pediatrician and cardiologist. Both tell me the same thing, it is probably a reaction to the steroids or antibiotics. I wait a few days, his stomach has not come down, if anything, it is bigger. I am concerned. Annette and I decide to take him to the emergency room. I hate hospitals, the smell and coldness makes me think of the past. I harbor too many bad memories that resurface when we arrive. Fear enters as we step through the automatic doors. John Paul's fear is greater than mine, I downplay the visit and promise no needles.

John Paul, Annette and I wait in a small room. Doctors and nurses come and go. Test and x-rays all come back negative. Adverse reaction to antibiotics or steroids is thought to be the cause. I am told to keep an eye on his condition if additional swelling appears or swelling around ankles is found, I am to bring him in or notify his doctor. I leave the hospital relieved that nothing major is the cause.

Months pass, John Paul's stomach does not get bigger, but it is still distended. Annette, John Paul and I take a trip up to North Carolina. One of my friends is playing in a PGA tournament and we are going to cheer him on. John Paul is ecstatic, he loves golf.

Dr. Reid Keever, Annette's obstetrician, and his family have become close friends. We all meet in Greensboro for dinner. I tell him about John Paul's distended stomach. He calls my son over and gives him a hug, casually examining his abdomen and then sends him off to play with his children.

"That's not normal."

I tell him the doctors diagnosis. He explains John Paul has been off of the medication long enough for it to be out of his system, something else has to be the cause of his swollen stomach. The worried look on his face makes me sick. I look at Annette who has been listening to our conversation.

"Is it serious?" She asks.

"That I do not know. Why don't you bring him to my office in the morning and I will ultrasound his abdomen."

Annette and I agree to meet at his office at nine-thirty in the morning.

The drive from Greensboro back to Annette's parent's home where we are staying is quiet. John Paul is asleep in the back seat. The last few years have been wonderful, complication free, now this. Something is not right. The concern in Reid's eyes flashes in and out of my mind.

John Paul questions why we are going to Uncle Reid's office. I tell him Uncle Reid wants to take a picture of his stomach and that it will not hurt. This doesn't faze him and he happily climbs on the table. John Paul is as cool as a cucumber, not me. The scan continues for twenty minutes, every inch of John Paul's abdomen is scanned. Afterwards, Annette takes John Paul to the car while I speak to Reid. He informs me that everything looks fine, but he is concerned as to the cause for the swollenness. He asks if he can call John Paul's pediatric cardiologist in Florida. I give him the number; he states he will be in touch after he speaks with the doctor.

I drop Annette and John Paul off at her parents', I have to meet my brother and collect golf tickets for some friends. On the way back I get a call from Annette, John Paul's doctor in Florida wants him to have blood work done immediately. I know Annette is petrified, so I tell her I will meet her at the diagnostic office.

I enter the office, the screams rip at my heart. His face is crimson red. His fists are clenched, he swings them uncontrollably like a boxer dazed and confused. Annette is sitting in a wood desk-like chair; John Paul is on her lap. My brother, Gerard, and I arrive within minutes of Annette's frantic call. The nurse, strapped with anxiety, stands in front of him, needle in hand.

"I won't hurt you, I promise," she says hoping to release his fear.

The words only make him scream louder. He has heard those words before and knows they are lies.

"He doesn't believe you. He knows it will hurt," I say walking over to John Paul. I kneel down in front of him, his sobs wheeze breathlessly. I look at Annette.

"What happened?"

"The nurse has had to stick him several times. She is unable to find a vein."

She pauses. "Should we leave? I can't put him through this."

I shake my head. "We do not have a choice, it has to be done." I glance up at the nurse. "One more try."

The nurse nods and prepares herself.

I grab my son's small arms. "John Paul you need to calm down." His fear-filled eyes lock with mine. "We have to do this. I need you to be a strong boy."

The nurse takes one step in his direction, he goes ballistic. It takes Annette, Gerard and I to restrain him as the nurse inserts the needle into his arm. His legs kick and body jerks, but within a few seconds the nurse shouts, "I got it!"

Early afternoon Dr. Keever calls with the results of the blood work. John Paul's protein levels are extremely low. Protein is vitally important because it builds, maintains and replaces tissues and organs; muscles and the immune system are all made up of mostly protein. Dr. Keever spoke to Dr. Bowen in Florida and he has requested that John Paul come in to see him as soon as possible.

Annette calls Dr. Bowen and schedules an appointment for tomorrow morning. We load up the SUV and head back to Florida. All the way, Annette and I rationalize. If he is losing protein then we will just have to feed him more foods rich in protein, hamburgers, cheese, and milk.

John Paul sits on the examining table, legs dangling waiting on Dr. Bowen. This is one doctor he doesn't mind coming to see, he knows Dr. Bowen does not allow needles in his office. He is still too young to comprehend all that is going on. The doctor enters the room. His normal wide smile is reduced, his usual upbeat and positive demeanor is guarded today.

Protein Losing Enthroperty, (PLE) a condition where protein is lost through the bowels or kidneys is the diagnosis. The next step, verify the source of the loss. Is protein being lost through the bowels or kidneys? I question if the medications, steroids and antibiotics could be a factor. Unlikely is the doctor's response. Dr. Bowen stuns Annette and I by saying PLE is a side effect of the

Norwood Procedure. In all the years John Paul has been living with his condition never once has anyone informed me of this possible side effect. After the visit, Annette phones Dr. Harmon to tell him about the complications. Furthermore, I am shock by his response. *You have to be very careful placing children who have had the Norwood Procedure on antibiotics.* Annette and I ponder. That being the case, why were we never told this vital information? In reality, Argumentin, the high-powered antibiotic given to John Paul could have triggered the PLE. What is worse? This entire complication may have been adverted if Annette and I had been warned about the hazards of antibiotics.

Once a week John Paul encounters the ordeal of blood work. Repetition does not lessen his fear and anxiety. Each visit is a carbon copy of the one in North Carolina. In the days and weeks that follow, it is discovered that John Paul is losing protein through his bowels. Although the news is not good, it is the lesser of the two evils. Losing protein through his kidneys would have been devastating.

I begin my mission to find ways to replenish John Paul's body with protein. The first thing I do is ask the doctor if he can take a protein supplement, a protein shake. With his permission I start John Paul on protein shakes, two a day, and make sure his diet is high in protein. It is a challenge, the shakes are bitter but my son is a trooper, plus Annette and I invent ways to spice them up. Unfortunately the protein settles in his stomach which means it is not filtering through his body. His stomach continues to become larger, it is noticeable and beginning to bother John Paul. Every time I look at him I am reminded of the ads on television of the malnourished children in Africa. Their fragile thin frames overshadowed by their swollen stomachs. People stare at him, some even comment on how large his stomach is. I am amazed at how inconsiderate the human race can be. The comments breed insecurity for John Paul, something hard to overcome. Every time I look at John Paul I am reminded of the statement, *It is important for John Paul to go to school, to interact with children his own age.* It is an easy statement to make if your son or daughter is healthy. For those who have a child with a disability, the agenda and daily life is different. It is a routine hard for others to comprehend. It is easy to talk the talk until you walk the walk. I learned the hard way, others no longer sway me, I follow my instincts guided by faith and prayer.

Four years I search the internet and phone every major medical facility hoping to find a drug, a remedy to help John Paul. God does work in mysterious ways. I am in Vegas doing a clothing show when one of my fellow reps introduces a new water, Enon. He says the water may benefit John Paul because it helps hydrate the cells. At this point I will try anything. I call Dr. Bowen and fax him the information on the water. He states the water will not harm John Paul and to give it a try. I start John Paul on the water. A couple of days later while reading the brochure I notice the name of a doctor from John Hopkins who helped develop the water. I phone and speak to his secretary. I explain John Paul's situation, she instantly puts the doctor on the line.

"Forget the water, I have a drug that will help your son."

His words spark hope. I give him Dr. Bowen's number. Within the hour Dr. Bowen calls in a prescription for Spironolactone. Within a week the fluid slowly begins to dissipate from John Paul's stomach, the difference is astonishing. Four years of not giving up prove beneficial. Like I stated previously, God works in mysterious ways. It is ironic that a bottle of water placed me on the path to finding the drug that helps John Paul.

The drug helps control the fluid retention, but his body continues to have problems absorbing the protein. The problem is counteracted by the high-protein diet he started four years ago, yet the PLE has slowed his growth. He is very small. Although he is thirteen, most people mistake him for an eight or nine year old and offer him a balloon at the grocery store or a sucker at the bank. A misconception that bruises his fragile confidence. It is a tough road for John Paul, not only from the medical perspective, but now a different obstacle appears as peer pressure begins to kick in. My protectiveness does not diminish but with each passing year I gradually begin to loosen the reins and let John Paul grow into the mold God made for him.

Chapter Fourteen

Gratitude

When it comes to life, the critical thing is whether you take things for granted or take them with gratitude.

Gilbert K. Chesterton

A smile that lights up my life

When I hear the word gratitude, I think of Annette's brother, Barry. I am blessed to be able to express my gratitude for Barry; it was not easy for him. Through a terrible debilitating disease, he became a prisoner in his own body, and lost the ability to speak. His mother, who he loved dearly, administered his every need. Verbally unable to thank his mother, Barry found a way to express his gratitude, through his engaging eyes. Gratitude is articulated in many ways, the love and gratitude Barry communicated by his emerald gaze was irrefutable.

I am fortunate to have this venue to convey my thanks. I have to admit I thought this last chapter would be the easiest to write; however, for some reason it has been difficult. The title itself is simple, gratitude, which is usually expressed with two simple words, thank you. In reality there is no way I can express my sincere gratitude to all those who have been involved in John Paul's life for the past thirteen years. There have been so many people who have come in and out of our lives during this timeframe. As I have mentioned many times, it is amazing how God places appropriate people in our lives at the appropriate times.

I believe people are sent into our lives for a purpose. I received an e-mail not long ago which made me think. People come into your life for a reason, a season or a lifetime. When someone enters your life for a reason, it is usually to meet a need. They may come to assist you during a difficult time to provide guidance, support, emotionally or spiritually. They may seem like a godsend. When our desire is fulfilled, their work done, the prayer you sent up answered, they move on. Some people come into your life for a season, because your turn has come to share, grow or learn. They may give you peace, make you laugh or teach you something. They give you unbelievable joy, but only for a season. Lifetime relationships teach you lifetime lessons. Things to build upon in order to have a solid emotional foundation. Your job is to accept the lesson, love the person and put the knowledge gained into other relationships and areas of your life. After reading this, I thought about all the people who entered my family's life in the past thirteen years. Some have been for a reason, a season and some a lifetime. It is because of each individual's unique love, friendship and prayer that John Paul is with us today. This chapter is dedicated to all the people who have nourished John Paul through prayer, kindness, love and dedication.

First and foremost I thank God for giving Annette and me our most precious gift, John Paul. If I were to say thank you every second of every day it would not be enough. It is only by the grace of God that John Paul lives. It is not only during the trying times that His presence is felt, it is on a daily basis. Annette feels that same presence. The presence intensifies when she sees a rainbow and is uplifted each time she hears "I Can See Clearly Now." This song has connected her and John Paul since hearing it on the way to the doctor's office. Our faith strengthens with every passing day. Sure there are valleys, but the valleys must be traveled in order to make it to the mountaintops.

I say thank you to the Blessed Mother for Her intercession. Thank you to all the guardian angels and saints, especially Saint Padre Pio whose presence was experienced on numerous occasions in some of our darkest hours with that sweet scent of a rose.

Writing this book I have relived events that have been secluded in the recesses of my mind for many years. Dredging these memories has been difficult; maybe that is why I waited so long. I did not impulsively one day say I am going to write a book about John Paul. It is much deeper than that. The memory is still vivid. During John Paul's hospital stay for the third stage, Annette and I were sitting on a cushioned bench in the breezeway of the Pediatric Intensive Care Unit floor. It was a down day. I began to think about John Paul and all the miracles that had taken place in his short life. I prayed for another miracle and in that prayer a vow was made. A vow to write a memoir of John Paul's life and share the many miracles God bestowed on him and my family.

During this journey I have come in contact with many families who are enduring the nightmare of having a sick child. I dedicate this book to each of you. Most not only have to deal with this dreadful nightmare, but also the day to day struggles of maintaining the family. I encourage anyone who is having a rough day, feeling desolate or down on their luck to visit the hospital. Take a walk down the corridors of the pediatric unit. See the children suffering with cancer, aids, heart problems or any illness. I guarantee after passing a few doors your attitude will change.

In life there are interruptions. There are simple interruptions, such as a cell phone ringing during dinner or a traffic jam, and there are serious interruptions. I have survived and am still surviving a serious interruption. Through the pages of this book I hope you have gained a positive perspective to always believe in hope even when you are told there is no hope. To never give up, to hold steadfast to faith, fortitude and perseverance. To remember the importance of being an advocate for those you love. Last but not least to embrace the precious and greatest gift of all, the gift of life. For life is a gift, one to be cherished and preserved.

Life with John Paul…

John Paul loving life

Three years have passed since the completion of John Paul's inspiring and amazing story. His birthday, a monumental one, sweet sixteen, just occurred. Hard to believe!

Plain and simple, life with John Paul is a blessing! Annette, John Paul and I try to begin each day by going to early morning mass. There is no better way to jump-start our day and John Paul loves going. He is the youngest in attendance and the older people love him. Most do not know of his past or his condition but somehow they sense he is special. I cannot count the times people have asked John Paul to pray for them, or say they see his future as a priest. I know John Paul is here for a reason and I accept whatever God wants of my son.

Kindergarten is the last time John Paul was in a formal school environment. The risk of sickness was too great. Hospital Homebound a program offered through the state of Florida provided John Paul with his education at home. A teacher came to our home for five hours a week. By the end of the third grade I began to realize more hours were needed in order to accomplish the required work. The problem, John Paul was required to meet the same curriculum standards as children attending school and receiving thirty plus hours a week, a chore virtually impossible. Annette inquired. The gentleman in charge of Hospital Homebound stated he was sorry, but John Paul happened to fall through the crack. He advised Annette to contact her Congressman and Senator. State officials, the Governor and the President were notified, all inquires and concerns fell on deaf ears. It is sad. Does No Child Left Behind not pertain to John Paul? And what about all the children, who, like John Paul have a disability that prevents them from attending school? These children should be afforded the same education as any other child. No disable or sick child should fall through 'the crack.' It is time our government steps up to the plate and makes sure that no child is really left behind. After a year, Annette and I realized we could not fight the system, so we relinquished our fight. We have taken matters in our own hands and presently home school John Paul.

Home schooling has allowed us to be able to travel, something John Paul loves to do. His first adventure just happened to be Disney World. I still remember the awe in his eyes the first time he saw Mickey Mouse and the entire Magic Kingdom. He was fascinated. All the people he had seen on television were now right in front of him signing autographs and shaking his hand. Dumbo was his favorite and after each ride he would go back in line and start over again. I could not wait to take him on It's A Small World, Peter Pan, and Snow White; however he did not want to go. He cried, kicked and screamed. He was petrified. I soon realized he was frightened to go on any ride which was dark.

I began to understand the affect the surgeries had on John Paul. He is afraid of dark places and loud noises. It even took awhile for him to adjust to the movie theater which no longer bothers him. Although it is not as bad today, he is still iffy of dark buildings, auditoriums and other similar places. Slowly Annette and I are chipping away this fear.

The next trip was Panama, where a good friend was getting married. I have to admit I was a little concerned taking him to Panama, but his cardiologist advised me to take him and let him experience life. Wow, what a wonderful time. John Paul watched ships pass through the Panama Canal, but I believe he enjoyed the wedding best of all. The evening wedding took place on a rooftop overlooking the ocean. John Paul, who has a passion for dancing, hit the dance floor with the first beat and did not stop until the band played the last song. What a thrill to see the smile stretched across his face as he enjoyed life to the fullest.

Next destination is Hawaii thanks to Make A Wish . This was not John Paul's first flight, however, it was his first extended flight. As we boarded the flight, the flight attendant asked John Paul if he would like to visit the cockpit and meet the captain. He gladly accepted the invitation and took a seat in the co-pilot's seat. That was just the beginning of an unbelievable trip. We normally fly coach. Inquisitive John Paul notices the benefits received by first class customers and always asks why we cannot fly first class. This trip we are informed our seats have been upgraded to first class. John Paul is ecstatic. He takes advantage of the situation by keeping the flight attendant busy with bringing him food, soda and movies.

John Paul loves history and is intrigued by the events which took place on December 7, 1941. The first place he wanted to visit, Ford Island and The Arizona Memorial. This attraction had a profound affect on John Paul; he spent hours exploring and reading the names of those who lost their lives on that day.

John Paul is a Food Network junkie; he loves to watch and experiment with recipes. Needless to say when he noticed Sam Choy's restaurant on the Big Island the car automatically turned in. When Mr. Choy came to our table and spoke to John Paul, well that was the icing on the cake. From that day forward, John Paul required us to eat one meal a day at Sam Choy's which was not a hard chore

considering the outstanding food. Diamond Head, the zoo, a submarine ride, scouting the North Shore and a day at the Polynesian Culture Center rounded our wonderful trip to Hawaii.

Cruising is the ultimate for John Paul; from his first cruise he was hooked. He likes the royal treatment, his every need catered to from the time he wakes up to the time he goes to bed. He loves being able to swim, hit golf balls, putt putt, play basketball, tennis and video games all on one big ship. Ports of call are an adventure for him. He enjoys experiencing diverse cultures and meeting new interesting people.

Like so many children, September 11th had a profound affect on John Paul. For months after the attack he drew pictures depicting the events of that day. John Paul is passionate and concerned for others. To this day he still speaks about those who lost their lives or were hurt. A few years back we went to New York City. The vision he had of the city was that etched in his mind from that horrific day. I wanted him to see New York City and realize the city is vibrant and alive. After visiting the St. Patrick's, Museum of Natural History, Times Square, Soho and the Statue of Liberty, John Paul's memory of New York City became a positive one.

My goal is take John Paul as many places as possible. We have done extensive traveling in the states allowing him to see the history of each community. I do regret I was not able to take him to Rome and have him blessed by Pope John Paul II. I hope in the near future Annette, John Paul and I will be able to travel to Rome, visit the grave of Pope John Paul II and receive a blessing from Pope Benedict.

John Paul is a happy child. He wakes every morning with a smile on his face. His laugh is contagious. He is sincere, thoughtful, kind and wise beyond his years when it comes to compassion. Many friends say he is an old soul, definitely not a child of his generation. He loves Styx, The Beatles, Paul McCartney, Michael Jackson, U2, ABBA, history, and he is a major movie buff.

As previously mentioned, John Paul loves the Food Network and does not hesitate to try new recipes out on me. Every morning at eleven he begins preparation for my lunch. I watch his small hands dice tomatoes, onions, cucumbers and whatever else he finds in the refrigerator. Next he adds spices, with this procedure he truly experiments, and then he separates the eggs and makes a marvelous egg white omelet. Before the plate is placed on the table he garnishes the plate for a perfect presentation. He anxiously awaits my response and the smile that brightens his face when I give a thumbs up approval is priceless.

Not only does John Paul love cooking, he loves his food. His day is scheduled by his meals. He cannot enjoy one meal from wondering what he will eat next. Annette and I are grateful he is a good eater because it has not always been that way. When he was small Annette and I would have to entertain him in order for him to eat. In other words we would have to distract him and then spoon the food into his mouth. Every meal was delivered outside while pushing him in a toy jeep, at the park or watching the planes take off and land at the community airport.

John Paul loves golf. Thankfully God bestowed him with a natural ability to play a sport that does not require too much physical exertion. His swing is effortless and he chips and putts like a champion. Club Pros and PGA Tour Players, who are friends of mine, comment on his exceptional ability.

Everyday is a golf day. I try to take John Paul to the driving range and to chip and putt. He is very dedicated and his dedication paid off. The first tournament he played in he won, and this past summer his golf coach placed him in a tournament with adults. Although the smallest of the seventy-five participants he was the most impressive. The adults enjoyed playing with John Paul and all were thrilled when his group finished fourth.

Not too long ago John Paul and I headed out to play a round of golf. This is a day I will never forget. It was a Thursday afternoon and John Paul was at the ninth tee, a par three. He hit a perfect shot and low and behold the ball went directly in the hole.

"I made a hole in one!" He jumps up and down, leaps to give me a hug and runs to the green.

We saved the ball and had it mounted. It now sits in a special place with his other golf trophies.

Golf has instilled other highlights in John Paul's life. Attending morning mass has allowed us to meet many gracious and kind people. One individual in particular, Don Smith, has been outstanding to John Paul. Through this kind gentleman, John Paul was able to meet and spend time with Jack Nicklaus. Mr. Nicklaus spent time with John Paul, gave him a tour of his office and showed him the background behind designing a golf course.

He also has a unique way of uplifting a down spirit. A few years back Annette was having a bad day. She remarked that the devil was really trying to hinder her from doing something which was good. She excused herself to go for a short walk. John Paul followed. She told me later that on her walk John Paul asked what was wrong. She explained to him that sometimes the harder we try to do good the more determined the devil becomes to stop us. She said John Paul looked up at her and said, "Mom, if the devil is riding your train then you need to get off."

She said she stopped, looked at him, and thought about the wisdom bundled inside her son. Then she told him, "You are right John Paul, I am going to ditch this train and take the next one."

John Paul loves being around family. I believe he is most happy when the house is full of family. For this reason he loves Thanksgiving, Christmas, New Years, Easter, Fourth of July and any event that brings the family together. He loves entertaining, telling stories and jokes.

His birthday is the highlight. This is his day to have a blast, do whatever he wants and eat whatever he wants. He plans his itinerary months in advance and informs every one of his plans.

John Paul is a big NFL football fan. Every Sunday during season the routine is the same. He anxiously waits for the paper to arrive. As soon as it hits the porch he is out the door retrieving the sports section. Next he gets his blue marker and circles his teams then he calls his football nemesis, Les the Banker, or better known as Uncle Les. The two converse over the phone about their teams and once the receiver is down, the game is on. At the end of the day the two get together and tally their wins and losses. Funny enough, John Paul's teams always seem to come out on top and he does not let 'Les the Banker' forget it.

In February 2007 John Paul got braces. I was apprehensive, I had heard the horror stories of children not being able to eat and the terrible pain and pressure associated with the braces. John Paul was so excited to have braces that I think he totally forgot about the pain. He actually looked forward to his orthodontic appointments. Being a teenager, I am positive it does not have anything to do with the young ladies who take care of him each visit.

Above are only snippets of John Paul's life since the surgery. The most important accomplishment of John Paul's life is that his suffering has helped other children. The doctors have used the research and treatment conducted on him to save others. Every mistake experienced by John Paul leads to a clearer pathway for those who suffer today. It is because of his endurance that lives are being saved.

Everyday with John Paul is an adventure. His zest for life is contagious. I wish I could bottle it up and give it to everyone.

I invite you to sneak a peek of John Paul today via YouTube. Please visit:

www.youtube.com/dukea2000

Life without John Paul, I cannot imagine. When I think of him, I think of this quote:

> *If you live to be hundred, I want to live to be a hundred minus one day so I never have to live without you.*
> —A.A. Milne

> *The reason why I wake up and I am happier than the previous day is because my kid is alive.*
> —Derek George

Family Photos

John Paul's grandparents

Annette's brother and sister who passed away,
John Paul's Uncle Barry and Aunt Debbie

John Paul's grandparents with his Uncle
Father Gary and Aunt Cecilia

John Paul's Uncle Gerard and Aunt Melissa

John Paul and his Uncle Les

John Paul's cousins

John Paul and his dog Issima